PHONICS THEY USE

Words for Reading and Writing

Third Edition

Patricia M. Cunningham
Wake Forest University

 **LONGMAN**

An imprint of Addison Wesley Longman, Inc.

New York • Reading, Massachusetts • Menlo Park, California • Harlow, England
Don Mills, Ontario • Sydney • Mexico City • Madrid • Amsterdam

Editor-in-Chief: Priscilla McGeehon
Senior Acquisitions Editor: Virginia L. Blanford
Marketing Manager: Wendy Albert
Full Service Production Manager: Eric Jorgensen
Project Coordination, Text Design, and Electronic Page Makeup: Electronic Publishing Services Inc., NYC
Cover Design Manager: Nancy Danahy
Cover Designer: Joel Zimmerman
Senior Print Buyer: Hugh Crawford
Printer and Binder: The Maple-Vail Book Manufacturing Group
Cover Printer: The Lehigh Press, Inc.

For permission to use copyrighted material, grateful acknowledgment is made to the copyright holders mentioned throughout this book, which are hereby made part of this copyright page.

Library of Congress Cataloging-in-Publication Data

Cunningham, Patricia Marr.
Phonics they use : words for reading and writing / Patricia M. Cunningham —3rd ed. p. cm.
   Includes bibliographical references and index.
   ISBN 0-321-02055-3
   1. Reading—Phonetic method.   I. Title
LB1573.3.C86 2000
372.46′5—dc21   99-15343
                                                              CIP

Please visit our website at http://www.awlonline.com

ISBN 0-321- 02055-3

2345678910—MA—020100

CONTENTS

PREFACE

W hat a difference ten years makes! When this book first appeared in 1991, very few reading gurus—my best friends included—gave it much of a chance. Phonics was not something you talked about, and most people believed (or pretended to believe) that teachers had stopped doing it. Somehow the first edition sold enough copies to allow it to be revised, and the second edition appeared just as people were beginning once again to talk about phonics. As this third edition appears, I hope we have regained some balance and common sense, and I hope this edition can help promote phonics as part of a good balanced reading program.

Readers of the first two editions will find some familiar activities here and quite a few new ones. In the past five years, I have become even more convinced that children all have their own learning personalities, and that variety in how we do phonics and spelling with children is critical if we are to teach all children to be fluent decoders and spellers.

The foundation chapter still emphasizes shared reading and writing as critical activities, and there is a new section on making and using predictable charts to help children develop print concepts and begin to learn some words, letter names, and sounds. It is clear that alphabet books and rhyming books play a big role in developing phonemic awareness, so the foundation chapter contains even more suggestions for using these two particularly helpful types of books.

Word walls have become commonplace—but many more classrooms have word walls than do word walls! In order for children who are not strong visual learners to learn to automatically read and spell these critical high-frequency words, we must do a variety of activities with these words.

Chapter 2 has lots of suggestions for ways to "do" word walls and ways to extend word-wall words to help with the spelling of many other words.

The theme of Chapter 3—Using Phonics and Spelling Patterns—is variety, transfer, and multilevelness. The activities provide ways to continue to develop phonemic awareness and basic letter-sound knowledge, and they give children opportunities to learn and use patterns to decode and spell words. As children Guess the Covered Word, they are constantly reviewing all the beginning sounds—and more importantly using these beginning sounds to figure out words that make sense and sound right. Rounding Up the Rhymes is an especially useful new activity since it begins with a book that has lots of rhyming words. Children are more apt to transfer their strategies to the books they are reading when some of the word activities originate in books. In Reading/Writing Rhymes lessons, children combine beginning letters with spelling patterns to produce lots of rhyming words they then use to write and read some silly rhymes. Using Words You Know activities have been redesigned to use popular brand names so that children learn how all the words they know can help them read and spell lots of other words.

Chapter Four emphasizes the need for children to learn to read and spell some big words so that they have in their heads examples for the patterns found in big words. Since children love to collect things, the emphasis in this chapter is on helping children become word collectors. Activities are suggested for class and personal collections. In addition to word collectors, children are encouraged to become word detectives, seeking out clues in words by comparing them to other words they know. Lots of prefix, suffix, and root word activities are suggested, and a new list—the Nifty Thrifty Fifty—is offered so that children can have an example for all the common prefixes, suffixes, and spelling changes.

The Research section has been updated to reflect all the interest and information that has been gathered about phonics since the current phonics frenzy began. The book ends with some tips for teachers who are faced with "The Phonics Test." Various versions of this are being given around the country, and as you will surely notice after reading this book, the jargon being tested has little to do with phonics anyone could use. Even if you are not going to be subjected to this test, you might want to look at the information here so that you will be able to interpret the headlines that scream, "Teachers can't teach phonics because they don't know phonics!"

ACKNOWLEDGMENTS

I would like to thank the following reviewers for their helpful suggestions:

Nancy Areglado, Tenafly School District, Tenafly, NJ
Jean Casey, California State University, Long Beach
Chris Cherrington, Bloomsburg University
Paula Costello, Williamsville Central School District, Williamsville, NY
Adrienne Herrell, California State University, Fresno
Nancy Horton, University of North Texas
Tim Shanahan, University of Illinois at Chicago
Elaine Stephens, Saginaw Valley State University
Pamela Terry Godt, Western Illinois University
Carolyn Walker, Ball State University

INTRODUCTION

"They know the skills. They just don't use them!" These words express the frustration felt by many teachers who spend endless hours teaching children phonics only to find that the skills demonstrated on a worksheet or a mastery test often don't get used where they matter—in reading and writing. Because poor readers have so much difficulty applying the phonics skills they learn, many experts have called for an end to phonics instruction: "Just let them read and write and they will figure out whatever they need to know." Now, everyone agrees that children must read and write; in fact, if you had to choose between teaching either phonics or reading and writing, you would always choose reading and writing. But you don't have to make a choice. You can engage the children's minds and hearts in reading good literature and finding their own voices as authors *and*, at the same time, teach them how our alphabetic language works.

All good readers have the ability to look at a word they have never seen before and assign it a probable pronunciation. Witness your ability to pronounce these made-up words:

bame   spow   perzam   chadulition

Of course, you weren't truly reading, because having pronounced these words, you didn't access any meaning. But if you were in the position of most young readers who have many more words in their listening-meaning vocabularies than in their sight-reading vocabularies, you would often meet words familiar in speech but unfamiliar in print. The ability you demonstrated to rapidly figure out the pronunciation of unfamiliar-in-print words would enable you to make use of your huge store of familiar-in-speech words and thus access meaning.

Before we go on, how did you pronounce the made-up word, *spow?* Did it rhyme with *cow* or with *snow?* Because the English language does not assign one sound to each letter, there are different ways to pronounce certain letter patterns, but the number of different ways is limited; moreover, with real words, unlike made-up words, your listening/speaking vocabulary lets you know which pronunciation to assign.

Not only do beginning readers use their phonics knowledge to enable them to read words they have not seen before, but this same knowledge also enables them to write. Had I dictated the four made-up words to you and asked you to write them, you would have spelled them in a way which is reasonably close to the way I spelled them. You might have spelled the first one *baim* and the last one *chedulition,* but your "invented" spelling would have resembled my made-up spelling to a remarkable degree.

All good readers and writers develop this ability to come up with pronunciations and spellings for words they have never read or written before. Many poor readers do not. Good readers and writers do, indeed, read and write, and as they read and write, they figure out how our system works. Poor readers and writers need to read and write, but they also need to have their attention directed to words and the way these words work, so that they can make rapid progress in reading and writing. This book is about how to direct children's attention toward letters and sounds to enable them to *use strategies,* not learn skills.

The distinction between strategy and skill is blurred, at best. But I would like to share with you how I distinguish them. To me, a strategy is something you do to accomplish some goal. People develop strategies to get things done, and often they don't have words to describe what they are doing. Strategies almost never have rules or jargon attached to them. Strategies are not usually something you know. Rather, they are something you *do!* Some examples might help to clarify this important distinction.

When good readers see a word they never before have seen in print, they stop momentarily and study the word by looking at every letter in a left-to-right sequence. As they look at all the letters, they are not thinking a sound for each letter, because good readers know that sounds are determined not by individual letters but by letter patterns. Good readers look for patterns of letters they have seen together before and then search their mental word stores looking for words with similar letter patterns. If the new word is a long word, they "chunk" it. That is, they put letters together that make familiar chunks.

Based on their careful inspection of the letters and their search through their mental store for words with the same letter patterns, good readers *try out* a pronunciation. They then go back and reread the sentence that contained the unfamiliar-in-print word and see if their pronunciation makes sense given the meaning they are getting from the context of surrounding words. If the pronunciation they came up with makes sense, they continue reading. If not, they look again at all the letters of the unfamiliar word and see what else would "look like this and make sense."

Imagine a young boy reading this sentence: *The man was poisoned by lead.* Now imagine that he pauses at the last word and then pronounces *lead* so that it rhymes with *bead.* His eyes then glance back, and he quickly rereads the sentence and realizes that "it doesn't sound right." He studies all the letters of *lead* again and searches for similar letter patterns in his mental word store. Perhaps he now accesses words such as *head* and *bread.* This gives him another possible pronunciation for this letter pattern. He tries this pronunciation, quickly rereads, realizes his sentence now "sounds right," and continues reading.

From this scenario, we can infer the strategies this good reader used to successfully decode an unfamiliar-in-print word:

1. Recognize that this is an unfamiliar word and look at all the letters in a left-to-right sequence.
2. Search your mental store for similar letter patterns and the sounds associated with them and come up with a probable pronunciation.
3. Reread the sentence to cross-check your probable pronunciation with meaning. If meaning confirms pronunciation, continue reading. If not, try again! Had this unfamiliar-in-print word been a big word, the reader would have had to use a fourth strategy:
4. Chunk the word by putting letters together which usually go together in the words you know.

These four strategies—looking at all the letters in a left-to-right sequence, matching letter patterns with pronunciation, chunking big words, and cross-checking—are supported by numerous research studies and by commonsense observations of what we, as good readers, do. (This is not a book about research, but this is a book based on research. The relevant research can be found at the end of this book.)

Now, with these strategies clearly in mind, let's briefly consider the purported phonics skills we teach children:

Sound out all the letters in the word, then blend them together to see what you have.

When an *a* is followed by a consonant and an *e,* try the long sound of *a.*

When there are two consonants that are not a digraph in the middle of a word, divide between them.

The second syllable of a three- or four-syllable word is often unaccented.

I could list many more, but these few examples should suffice. Poor readers don't use such skills because they do not represent the strategies good readers use. Rather, the listed skills are an attempt to describe our system and explain it. The strategies are what you do when you come to a word you don't recognize or can't spell. Strategies are mental processes you use to do something you want to do. Some good readers learn these strategies—on their own—from their reading and writing, without (and sometimes in spite of) our instruction, but many children don't. They never figure out how you do it! They sound every letter and then can't blend what they have. They try to remember what the *e* does to the *a* and whether those two consonants in the middle are a digraph, but then they don't know what to do with that knowledge. This book is written for those children and for teachers who want to teach those children.

The book describes activities that I and numerous teachers have used to help children who have not figured out the strategies on their own and who don't know "what you do!" In writing this book and in developing and collecting the activities to include, I have tried to follow these five principles:

1. Because children are "active" learners, they should not just sit and listen or watch but should be actively engaged in doing something.
2. Because children are at all different stages in their word knowledge, a good activity has to be multilevel—have "something for everyone." All the activities in *Phonics They Use* have various things you can learn from the same activity, depending on what you are ready to make sense of.
3. Because children have different personalities, learning preferences, and ways in which they learn most easily, activities include as much variety as possible—chanting, singing, rhythm, rhyme, drama, movement, games, and so on.
4. Jargon and rules should be kept to the absolute minimum required to communicate.
5. The sole purpose for learning to decode and spell words is to enable reading and writing. All activities stress transfer to reading and writing. Phonics activities are short and focused so that children spend the vast majority of their language arts time engaged in real reading and writing.

There are four chapters in this book. Chapter 1 details the incredibly large amount of information brought to school by children who come from homes in which literacy is a priority. More importantly, this first chapter describes activities that real teachers working with real children have used in trying to make sure all children have the foundation needed to learn to read and write. Although Chapter 1 will be particularly useful to preschool and kindergarten teachers, first- and second-grade teachers who have children who are not making progress in reading and writing often need to include some of these foundational activities in their classrooms.

Because English contains numerous irregular words—those not pronounced or spelled in the way you would expect them to be—and because these irregular words are also the most common words, Chapter 2 describes specific activities you can use with children to speed them along the route to immediate and automatic recognition and spelling of such highly frequent words.

Chapter 3 describes activities for helping children learn to decode and spell regular one- and two-syllable words. Activities help children learn all the beginning letters—consonants, blends, and digraphs—and how to combine these beginning letters with spelling patterns to decode and spell thousands of words.

Chapters 2 and 3 will be most useful to first- and second-grade teachers; those who teach older children who lack strategies in decoding and spelling will find these strategies also work for older children.

Chapter 4 is devoted to the special problems some students experience as they encounter multisyllabic, or *big*, words in their reading and writing. The chapter describes a variety of activities for helping children become independent with big words. These activities are probably most on target for average third and fourth graders but have been used by middle and even high school teachers of students with bigwordphobia. Of course, remedial reading teachers will need to pick and choose age-appropriate activities throughout the book.

Finally, because I believe that teachers want to know the why behind the how, I have included a summary of the research base underlying the activities found in *Phonics They Use*. This research summary should provide teachers with an understanding of why the book includes such a variety of activities and how these activities promote decoding and spelling fluency for a wide variety of readers.

1

THE FOUNDATION FOR PHONICS THEY CAN USE

Before we begin helping children learn letter-sound relationships they can use, we must be sure our children know what they are trying to learn and how it is useful to them. Currently, we have a tremendous amount of research, usually included under the term *emergent literacy* (Teale & Sulzby, 1991), which shows us what happens in the homes of children where literacy is a priority. We know that children born into homes where someone spends time with them in reading and writing activities walk into our schools with an incredible foundation on which our instruction can easily build. These children experience an average of over 1,000 hours of quality one-on-one reading and writing activities.

Parents, grandparents, aunts, uncles, and babysitters read to children and talk with them about what they are reading. This reading is usually done in the *lap position,* where the child can see the pictures as well as the words used to tell about the pictures. Favorite books are read time and again, and eventually most children opt for a book which they *pretend-read*—usually to a younger friend or a stuffed animal.

In addition to reading, these children are exposed to writing at an early age. They scribble and make up ways to spell words. They ask (and are told) how to spell favorite words. They make words from their magnetic letters and copy favorite words from books. From the over 1,000 hours of reading and writing experiences, these children learn some incredibly important concepts.

CONCEPTS YOUNG CHILDREN LEARN FROM READING-WRITING ENCOUNTERS

What Reading and Writing Are For

Imagine you are visiting in a first-grade classroom. You have a chance to talk with several children and ask them, "Why are you learning to read and write?" Some children answer, "You have to learn to read and write." When pushed, they can name all kinds of real-world products as reasons for reading and writing—books, newspapers, magazines, recipes, and maps. Other children respond to the why-learn-to-read-and-write question with answers such as, "to do your workbook," "to read in reading group," and "to go to second grade." Children who give school-world answers to this critical question demonstrate that they don't see reading and writing as part of their real world. Children who don't know what reading is for in the real world do not have the same drive and motivation as children for whom reading and writing, like eating and sleeping, are things everyone does. In addition, children who pretend-read a memorized book and "write" a letter to grandma are confident they can read and write!

Print Concepts

Print is what you read and write. Print includes all the funny little marks—letters, punctuation, space between words and paragraphs—that translate into familiar spoken language. In English, we read across the page in a left-to-right fashion. Because our eyes can see only a few words during each stop (called a fixation), we must actually move our eyes several times to read one line of print. When we finish that line, we make a return sweep and start all over again, left to right. If there are sentences at the top of a page and a picture in the middle and more sentences at the bottom, we read the top first and then the bottom. We start at the front of a book and go toward the back. These arbitrary rules about how we proceed through print are called *conventions*. Other languages have other conventions for getting through print. Hebrew, for example, is read from back to front, and Chinese is read from top to bottom in columns. Successful readers understand the conventions of print of their language.

Jargon refers to all the words we use to talk about a particular activity or area of interest. The jargon we use to talk about reading and writing includes such terms as *word*, *letter*, *sentence*, and *sound*. We use this jargon constantly as we try to teach children how to read:

> "Look at the **first word** in the **second sentence**. How does that **word begin**? What **letter** has that **sound**?"

Using some jargon is essential to talking with children about reading and writing, but children who don't come from rich literacy backgrounds are often very confused by this jargon. Although all children speak in words, they don't know words exist as separate entities until they are put in the presence of reading and writing. To many children, letters are what you get in the mailbox, sounds are horns and bells and doors slamming, and sentences are what you have to serve if you get caught committing a crime. These children are unable to follow our "simple" instructions because we are using words for which they have no meaning or an entirely different meaning.

Many children come to school knowing these print concepts. From being read to in the lap position, they have noticed how the eyes "jump" across the lines of print as someone is reading. They have watched people write grocery lists and thank-you letters to Grandma and have observed the top-bottom, left-right movement. Often, they have typed on the computer and observed these print conventions. Because they have had someone to talk with them about reading and writing, they have learned much of the jargon.

While writing down a dictated thank-you note to Grandma, Dad may say, "Say your sentence one word at a time if you want me to write it. I can't write as fast as you can talk." When the child asks how to spell *birthday*, he may be told, "It starts with the letter *b*, just like your dog Buddy's name. *Birthday* and *Buddy* start with the same sound and the same letter."

Children with reading and writing experiences know how to look at print and what teachers are talking about as they give them information about print. All children need to develop these critical understandings in order to learn to read and write.

Phonemic Awareness

The ability to recognize that words are made up of a discrete set of sounds and to manipulate sounds is called *phonemic awareness,* and children's level of phonemic awareness is very highly correlated with their success in beginning reading (Lundberg, Frost, & Petersen, 1988; Hoffman, Cunningham, Cunningham, & Yopp, 1998). Phonemic awareness develops through a series of stages during which children first become aware that language is made up of individual words, that words are made up of syllables, and that syllables are made up of phonemes. It is important to note here that it is not the "jargon" children learn. Five-year-olds cannot tell you there are three syllables in *dinosaur* and one syllable in *Rex*. What they can do is clap out the beats in *dinosaur* and the one beat in *Rex*. Likewise, they cannot tell you that the first phoneme in *mice* is *m*, but they can tell you what you would have if you took the *mmm* off *mice*: *ice*. Children develop this phonemic awareness as a result of the oral and written language they are exposed to. Nursery rhymes, chants, and Dr. Seuss books usually play a large role in this development.

Phonemic awareness is an oral ability. You hear the words that rhyme. You hear that *baby* and *book* begin the same. You hear the three sounds in *bat* and can say these sounds separately. Only when children realize that words can be changed and how changing a sound changes the word are they able to profit from instruction in letter-sound relationships.

Children also develop a sense of sounds and words as they try to write. In the beginning, many children let a single letter stand for an entire word. Later, they put more letters and often say the word they want to write, dragging out its sounds to hear what letters they might use. Children who are allowed and encouraged to "invent spell" develop an early and strong sense of phonemic awareness.

Some Concrete Words

If you sit down with first graders on the first day of school and try to determine if they can read by giving them a simple book to read or testing them on some common words such as *the, and, of,* or *with,* you would probably conclude that most first graders can't read yet. But many first graders can read and write some words. Here are some words a boy named David knew when he began first grade:

David
Mama
Daddy
Bear Bear (his favorite stuffed animal)
Carolina (his favorite basketball team)
Pizza Hut
I love you (written on notes on good days)
I hate you (written on notes on bad days)

Most children who have had reading and writing experiences have learned 10 to 15 words. The words they learn are usually concrete words important to them. This knowledge is important, not because they can read much with these few words, but because children who come to school already able to read or write some concrete words have accomplished an important and difficult task. They have learned how to learn words.

Some Letter Names and Sounds

Finally, many children have learned some letter names and sounds. They can't usually recognize all 26 letters in both upper- and lowercase, and they often don't know the sounds of *w* or *c*, but they have learned the names and sounds for the most common letters. Usually, the letter names and sounds children know are based on those concrete words they can read and write.

The Foundation

From the research on emergent literacy, we finally understand what we mean when we say a child is "not ready." We know that many children have hundreds of hours of literacy interactions during which they develop understandings critical to their success in beginning reading. We must now structure our school programs to try to provide for all children what some children have had. This will not be an easy task. We don't have 1,000 hours, and we don't have the luxury of doing it with one child at a time, and when the child is interested in doing it! But we must do all we can, and we must do it in ways that are as close to the home experiences as possible. In the remainder of this chapter, I describe activities successfully used by kindergarten and first-grade teachers who are committed to putting all children in the presence of reading and writing and allowing all children to learn:

What reading and writing are for
Print concepts
Phonemic awareness
Some concrete words
Some letter names and sounds

For older children just acquiring English, these understandings are also critical for them to develop the foundation on which reading and writing can grow.

SHARED READING OF PREDICTABLE BOOKS

Teachers of young children have always recognized the importance of reading a variety of books to children. There is one particular kind of book and one particular kind of reading, however, that has special benefits for building the reading and writing foundations—shared reading with predictable Big Books.

Shared reading is a term used to describe the process in which the teacher and the children read a book together. The book is read and reread many times. On the first several readings, the teacher usually does all of the reading. As the children become more familiar with the book, they join in and "share" the reading.

The best books to use with shared reading are predictable books. Predictable books are books in which repeated patterns, refrains, pictures, and rhyme allow children to pretend-read a book that has been read to them several times. Pretend reading is a stage most children go through with a favorite book that some patient adult has read and reread to them. Perhaps you remember pretend reading with such popular predictable books as *Goodnight Moon, Are You My Mother?* or *Brown Bear, Brown Bear.* Shared reading of predictable books allows all children to experience this pretend reading. From this pretend reading, they learn what reading is, and they develop the confidence that they will be able to do it. They also develop print concepts and begin to understand how letters, sounds, and words work.

In choosing a book for shared reading, consider three criteria. First, the book must be very predictable. The most important goal for shared reading is that even children with little experience with books and stories will be able to pretend-read the book after several readings and develop the confidence that goes along with that accomplishment. Thus, you want a book without too much print and one in which the sentence patterns are very repetitive and the pictures support those sentence patterns.

Second, you want a book that will be very appealing to the children. Since the whole class of children will work with the same Big Book, and since the book will be read and reread, you should try to choose a book that many children will fall in love with.

Finally, the book should take you someplace conceptually. Many teachers choose Big Books to fit their units, build units around the books, or share Big Books by the same author or illustrator to study style.

The teacher and children are doing a shared reading of a predictable book.

When engaging in shared reading with predictable Big Books, we try to simulate what would happen in the home as a child delights in having a favorite book read again and again. First, we focus on the book itself, on enjoying it, rereading it, talking about it, and acting it out. As we do this, we develop concepts and oral language. When most of the children can pretend-read the book, we focus their attention on the print. We do writing activities related to the book and help children learn print conventions, jargon, and concrete words. When children know some concrete words, we use these words to begin to build phonemic awareness and letter-sound knowledge.

Here is an example of shared reading using the ever popular *Hattie and the Fox* by Mem Fox. In this book, Hattie, a big black hen, notices something in the bushes:

> "Goodness gracious me!
>
> I can see a nose in the bushes!"

The other animals respond:

> "Good grief," said the goose.
>
> "Well, well," said the pig.
>
> "Who cares?" said the sheep.
>
> "So what?" said the horse.
>
> "What next?" said the cow.

The teacher and children are sharing the reading of *Hattie and the Fox*.

As the story continues, Hattie sees a nose and two eyes in the bushes, then a nose, two eyes, and two ears. Next two legs appear, followed by a body and two more legs. As Hattie announces each new sighting, the other animals respond with the same lack of concern. But when Hattie announces it is a fox, the other animals respond:

> "Oh, no!" said the goose.
>
> "Dear me!" said the pig.
>
> "Oh, dear!" said the sheep.
>
> "Oh, help!" said the horse.
>
> But the cow said "MOO!"

This frightens the fox away, and the animals go on about their business.

Read and Talk About the Book

Observational research of children being read to shows that parents not only read to children but engage the children in conversation about the book and reread favorite books. We try to promote this kind of conversation and interaction as each book is read. After reading the first two pages, the teacher would encourage predictions by asking,

> "What do you think Hattie sees?"

Children would be encouraged to infer character feelings by responding to questions such as,

> "Why do the other animals say things like 'who cares?' and 'so what?'"

As the book continues and more body parts are revealed, children express their annoyance with the unconcerned animals:

> "They should figure out it is a fox!"

and their fear that

> "They'd better watch out. That fox could eat them!"

As with any book, the first and second reading of a Big Book should be strictly focused on the meaning and enjoyment of the book. *Hattie and the Fox* has delightful illustrations, and children will enjoy the suspense of watching the fox emerge.

Encourage the Children to Join in the Reading

There are a variety of ways to encourage children to join in. For *Hattie and the Fox,* children will almost naturally want to say the repeated responses of the animals and join Hattie in adding the body parts as she sees them. You might also want to "echo read" the book, with you reading each line and then the children being your echo and reading it again. Some teachers like to practice and then make a tape recording in which the teacher reads some parts and the whole class or groups of children read the words of the various animals. Children delight in going to the listening center and listening to themselves reading the book.

Act It Out

Young children are natural actors. They pretend and act out all kinds of things. They don't need props or costumes, but you may want to make some simple line drawings of the animals (with several showing the parts of the fox as it emerges). If you punch two holes and put yarn through and laminate these, children can wear the cards around their necks and everyone will know who they are. Act it out several times, letting everyone have a chance to be one of the animals or a part of the fox. Read the part that is not repetitive, and let children in the audience read the repetitive parts with you.

Let the Children Match Sentence Strip Sentences and "Be the Words"

Write some of the sentences—probably the repeated responses of the animals—on sentence strips. Let children put them in the right order by matching them to the same sentences in the book and arranging them in a pocket chart. Have children read from the sentence strips. Next, let the children watch

These children are ready to act out *Hattie and the Fox*.

These children are being the words for the popular predictable book
Brown Bear, Brown Bear, What Do You See?

you cut some sentences into words. Mix up the words and have them recreate the book page from the words. Children enjoy manipulating the words, and it is excellent practice for left-to right, top-to-bottom print tracking.

Decide What You Notice About the Letters and Words

Choose some sentences from the book, perhaps these:

"Good grief," said the goose.

"Well, well," said the pig.

"Who cares?" said the sheep.

"So what?" said the horse.

"What next?" said the cow.

Ask the children to look at these sentences and come up and point out what they notice. Children will notice a variety of things depending on their level. These will probably include:

"Good, grief, and *goose* begin with a *g."*

"Pig has a *g* too, but it is at the end."

"Said is in every sentence—five times!"

"The is also there five times!"

"What is there two times."

"The *What* in the last sentence has a capital *W."*

"All the sentences have these things." (pointing to quotation marks)

"These three sentences have question marks."

"The first two sentences have these." (pointing to exclamation marks)

Whatever the children notice is accepted and praised by the teacher. The teacher also asks more questions:

"Does anyone know what these marks are called? Why are they there?"

And offers explanations:

"That is called a question mark and those animals are all asking questions."

"Good noticing. That *What* has a capital *W* because it is the first word in the sentence."

Once the book has been read, enjoyed, reread, acted out, and had some attention focused on the sentences, words, and letters, most children will be able to read (or pretend-read) most of the book. This early "I Can Read" confidence is critical to emerging readers, and the shared book experience as described is a wonderful way to foster this.

Develop Print Concepts by Pointing Out Features of the Book

Make sure children can find the front and back of the book as well as the title and author's name. Have individual children come and point to words as everyone reads to make sure they know that the words are what you read and that you move in a left-right fashion across each line of print. Have children use their hands to show you just one word, the first word in a sentence, the last word, the longest word, and so forth.

Develop Phonemic Awareness, Letter-Sound Connections, and Concrete Words

One critical component of phonemic awareness is the ability to hear when words start with the same sound. Once children can distinguish when words begin alike, they can begin to learn which letters make which sounds. Letter sounds, like other learnings, can be learned by rote or by association. Learning the common sound for *h* by trying to remember it or by trying to remember that it begins the words *hen* and *horse* when you can't read the words *hen* and *horse* requires rote learning. Once you can read the words *hen* and *horse* and realize that the common sound for *h* is heard at the beginning of *hen* and *horse*, you no longer have to just remember the sound. You can now associate the sound of *h* with something already known, the words *hen* and *horse*. Associative learning is the easiest, quickest, and longest lasting.

Children from print-rich environments know some concrete words when they come to school. As they are taught letter-sounds, they probably associate these with the words they know, thus making the learning of these sounds easier and longer lasting. We can provide this opportunity for associative learning for children who did not know words when they came to school by capitalizing on the words they have learned from *Hattie and the Fox.*

The number of letter-sounds you wish to focus on from one book will depend on what your children already know and on what words are available in the book. Choose words that have clear initial sounds and that most of the children have learned through the multiple activities you have done with the book. The words *Hattie, hen,* and *horse* are all important words and, they give children three connections for the sound of *h. Goose, cow,* and *fox* are clear examples for *g, c,* and *f.*

Regardless of how many letter-sounds you teach using the key words, the procedure should be the same. Begin with two letters that are very different in look and sound and that are made in different places in the mouth—*h* and *c,* for example. Show the children the words—*Hattie, hen, horse,* and *cow*—that will serve as key words for these letters. Tell the children to pronounce the key words and to notice the position of their tongues and teeth as they do. Say several concrete words (*car, hat, hop, cat, hug, cup, corn*) that begin like *Hattie, hen, horse,* and *cow,* and have the children say them after you. Have them notice where their tongue and teeth are as they say the words. Let the children point to and say the key words to indicate how the word begins.

Begin a key-word bulletin board on which you put the letters *h* and *c* and the key words *Hattie, hen, horse,* and *cow.* Repeat the activity just described using other *h* and *c* words until most of the children begin to understand the difference in the letter-sound. Then add a third letter and key word—perhaps *f* and *fox.* Have them listen for and repeat words beginning with all three letters—*h, c,* and *f.* Be sure to point out that the words they already know will help them remember the sounds. You could then add in a fourth letter and key word—*g* and *goose.*

Making this key-word bulletin board is a multilevel activity. Multilevel means that there are multiple things to be learned through the same activity—depending on what you are ready to learn. By having children listen to words and decide if they begin like *Hattie, fox, cow,* or *goose,* you are helping those who still need to develop the phonemic awareness sense of which words sound alike at the beginning. When you help them notice that these letters are *h, f, c,* and *g,* you are helping them establish letter-sound connections we call phonics. Children must develop phonemic awareness in order to learn phonics. This multilevel activity has "something for everyone."

Develop Concepts of Rhyme and Phonemic Awareness.

Another component of phonemic awareness is the ability to hear when words rhyme. Once children can hear rhymes, they can read rhyming words by changing the beginning sound and making the word rhymes. Three of the concrete words in *Hattie and the Fox*—*hen*, *pig,* and *sheep*—have lots of words that rhyme and are spelled with the same pattern. Here is an activity you can use to help develop both the ability to hear rhyme—phonemic awareness—and the ability to read new rhyming words by changing the initial letter—phonics.

Show the children the words *hen*, *pig,* and *sheep,* which most of the children should recognize by now. Tell them that you are going to say words that rhyme with one of the animals. Their job is to repeat the word you say and then say the animal names to decide which one rhymes. Say some common words that rhyme, such as *big, ten, jeep, beep, men, dig, wig, pen, keep.* Have the children decide which word these new words rhyme with. Once they have decided, write the new word under the rhyming word, stretching out the word and letting the children help you decide what letter they hear at the beginning. Your list should look like this:

<u>hen</u>	<u>pig</u>	<u>sheep</u>
ten	big	jeep
men	dig	beep
pen	wig	keep

When you have this list completed, have the children read each group of rhyming words, and help them notice that the beginning letter is different but the rest of the word has the same pattern.

This activity, like the preceding one with beginning sounds, is multilevel. Children who still need to develop the oral concept of rhyme have a wonderful opportunity to do so. Other children can begin to see how you read words by blending a beginning sound you know with a pattern you recognize from other rhyming words.

Shared Reading With Poems, Songs, and Chants

In addition to books, many teachers write favorite poems, chants, songs, and finger plays on long sheets of paper, and these become some of the first things children can actually read. Most teachers teach the poem, chant, song, or finger play to the children first. Once the children have learned to say, chant, or sing it, they then are shown what the words look like. The progression to reading is a natural one, and children soon develop the critical "Of course I can read" self-confidence. Once children can read the piece, many teachers copy it and send it home for the child to read to parents and other family members.

How Shared Reading Develops the Crucial Understandings

Shared reading can be used to develop all of the crucial understandings. Children develop left-right, top-bottom print conventions as they read with you and when they reassemble words to make sentences. They also understand that words make up sentences. When they compare the sounds of different parts of different words, they begin to understand that letters represent sounds. Through all these activities, they firm up their understanding of critical jargon—words, sentences, letters, sounds. When reading a predictable Big Book is extended by word and letter-sound activities, children learn some concrete words, letter names, and sounds, and they increase phonemic awareness. Of course, children learn that one of the reasons we read is to enjoy wonderful books such as *Hattie and the Fox*. Shared reading also promotes "I can't wait" and "I can do it" attitudes.

SHARED WRITING OF PREDICTABLE CHARTS

Just as children enjoy reading predictable books together, they also like to write and read predictable charts. Writing a predictable chart is a natural follow-up to a predictable book, a field trip, or a new topic or theme. *Things I Like* by Anthony Browne is about a little chimp who tells about all the things he likes ("This is me and this is what I like: Painting . . . and riding my bike. Playing with toys, and dressing up"). It is the pictures in this book that make the book predictable, not the pattern.

After reading and enjoying *Things I Like*, talk with the children about things they like and then record these on a Things I Like chart. Begin by putting the title on the top line of a large sheet of lined chart paper. (Usually, *Things I Like* is chosen for the title of the chart also.) As you write the title, say each word and the letters in each word so that children will watch both left to right progression and letter formation. Next, write what you—the teacher—like to do.

I like reading books. (Miss Williams)

Next, ask each child to tell something they like or like to do. Write their sentences on the chart and place each child's name after the sentence with parentheses around their name separating it from the sentence. This is what the finished chart might look like:

Things I like
I like reading books. (Miss Williams)
I like swimming. (Michelle)
I like eating french fries. (Jasmine)
I like pizza. (Suzanne)
I like computers. (Ryan)
I like running. (Adam)
I like playing football. (Refugio)
I like riding my bike. (William)
I like playing basketball. (Erica)
I like making cookies. (Olivia)
I like going to the beach. (Mike)
I like making cookies. (Nikki)
I like watching TV. (Paul)
I like playing with my friends. (Mitchell)
I like soccer. (Jacob)
I like school. (Emily)
I like my Barbie dolls. (Julie)
I like going to the mall. (Rashawn)
I like my teacher. (Tiarra)
I like reading books. (Cindy)
I like drawing pictures. (Christopher)
I like centers. (Paul)
I like computer games. (Mitchell)
I like school. (Richard)

When the predictable chart is completed, the teacher reads it to the children or has children read their own sentences to the class. Children can do this because they know each sentence starts with "I like . . ." and finishes with what they said.

Decide What You Notice About the Letters and Words

On the following day, have the children read the predictable chart, *Things I Like*, again, with children reading their own sentences. When you finish, ask the children to look at the sentences and come up and point to things they notice. Children will notice a variety of things, depending on what they know about letters, sounds, words, and reading. These may include:

"All sentences begin with *I Like.*"

"*French* and *fries* begin with the same two letters, 'fr.'"

"*Ryan* and *Refugio* both start with an 'R.'"

"*I* is at the beginning of each sentence."

"*I* is always a capital letter."

"Lots of words have 'ing' at the end."

"*TV* is spelled with two letters, 'T' and 'V.'"

"All sentences have this (a period) at the end."

Whatever the children notice is accepted and praised by the teacher. The teacher also asks more questions—"Does anyone know what this mark is called? Why is it placed there?"—and offers explanations: "That is called an exclamation mark; it is placed there to show that the teacher really likes her class and is excited about them." "Good noticing! *TV* is made up of two letters. Does anyone know what kind of letters those are?" Another activity the children like to do is to act out their sentence. By reading the names on the chart, the children will know whose turn is next.

Sentence Builders (Being the Words)

On another day, write the first sentence from the *Things I Like* chart on a sentence strip with a thick black magic marker. Have a child find the first sentence on the chart and match the sentence strip to it. Do this for several of the sentences on your predictable chart. Next, let the children watch you cut the first sentence into words. Mix up the words for this sentence and have them recreate the sentence from the words in your pocket chart, just as it is on the first line of your predictable chart. Then, let the children be the words and build the sentence. Give the words to the children. (The child whose sentence is being made gets his or her name.) Let the children stand in front of the class in the same order as the words in the first sentence on the chart. Have the class read the sentence after all children are lined up in the sentence order. Repeat this procedure for the second sentence, taking the words and giving those words to different children. Ask them to become "sentence builders" and to get in the right order, so that they look like the second sentence on the chart. When the children get in their places, have everyone read the sentence. Continue with as many sentences as you have time for.

Making a Class Book

The final activity for each predictable chart is creating a class book. Have the children reread the predictable chart again; then give each child an envelope with his or her cut-up sentence inside. Have each child sequence the words to make the sentence on the bottom of a piece of drawing paper. Check their sentences and then have the children paste the words in their sentence on the paper. Next, the children take crayons or colored markers and illustrate their sentences. Finally, these pages are put together into a class book which the teacher and the children read together.

How Predictable Charts Develop the Crucial Understandings

Young children are very egocentric, and predictable charts capitalize on this. Children love the predictable charts and class books because they are all about them! They will tell you that if you read this book, you can find out what they all like to do—a clear and important purpose for reading and writing. When writing a predictable chart, there are many different things for young children to notice. Children with little print experience learn

Here are children being the words for one of the "I like . . ." sentences.

Here are some class books one class made from their predictable charts.

what reading is and begin to develop "concepts of print." They learn that each sentence starts at the left and goes to the right. They see the teacher start at the top and go the bottom. They hear the teacher talk about "words," "sentences," and "letters" and learning about these things. Having the children "be" the words, cutting sentences into words and rearranging them, and making new sentences from familiar words all help children understand what words are. Making predictable charts is a multilevel activity through which children who lack reading and writing experiences can build critical understandings, and children who come to school with these understandings can usually read the whole chart. Most children learn a few words and begin to notice how words are the same and different. If you use these words most children learn as key words, you can build letter-sound concepts on these words, as was described for the key words from *Hattie and the Fox*. Perhaps most important, all children develop the desire to learn to read and the confidence that they *are* learning to read.

WRITING

Until recently, kindergarten and first-grade children were often not allowed or encouraged to write until they could make most of the letters correctly and spell lots of words. The theory was that if children were allowed to

Predictable charts made during a unit on friends and zoo animals.

write before they could spell and make the letters correctly, they would acquire "bad habits" that later would be hard to break. There is a certain logic in this argument, but it does not hold up to scrutiny when you actually look at children before they come to school.

Just as children from literacy-oriented homes read before they can read by pretend-reading a memorized book, they write before they can write! Their writing is usually not readable by anyone besides themselves, and sometimes they read the same scribbling different ways. They write with pens, markers, crayons, paint, chalk, and with normal-sized pencils with erasers on the ends. They write on chalkboards, magic slates, walls, drawing paper, and lined notebook paper. (They just ignore the lines.) They write in scribbles, which first go anywhere and then show a definite left-to-right orientation. They make letterlike forms. They underline certain letters to show word boundaries. As they learn more about words and letters, they let single letters stand for entire words. They draw pictures and intersperse letters with the pictures. They make grocery lists by copying words off packages. They copy favorite words from books.

Emergent literacy research has shown us that children are not ruined by being allowed to write before they can write. Rather, they learn many important concepts and develop the confidence that they can write (Sulzby, Teale, & Kamberelis, 1989). Here are some activities that promote writing for all.

Provide a Print-Rich Classroom

Classrooms in which children write contain lots of print. In addition to books, there are magazines and newspapers. Charts of recipes tried and directions for building things hang as reminders. Children's names are on their desks and on many different objects. There are class books, bulletin boards with labeled pictures of animals under study, and labels on almost everything. Children's drawings and all kinds of writing are displayed. In these classrooms, children see that all kinds of writing are valued. Equally important, children who want to write "the grown-up way" can find lots of words to make their own.

Let Children Watch You Write

As children watch you write, they observe that you always start in a certain place, go in certain directions, and leave space between words. In addition to these print conventions, they observe that writing is "talk written down." There are numerous opportunities in every classroom for the teacher to write as the children watch—and sometimes help—with suggestions of what to write.

Language experience is a time-honored practice in which the teacher records the children's ideas. Language experience can take the form of a group-dictated chart, which may list what the class learned about monkeys, or an individually dictated sentence recorded at the bottom of a child's picture. Language experience takes place whenever a child's words are recorded so the child can see that writing is truly a permanent record of speech. Predictable charts are a particular kind of language experience, and in fact, for years we called the making of predictable charts "structured language experience."

In many classrooms, the teacher begins the day by writing a morning message on the board. The teacher writes this short message as the children watch. The teacher then reads the message, pointing to each word and inviting the children to join in on any words they know. Sometimes, teachers take a few minutes to point out some things students might notice from the morning message:

"How many sentences did I write today?"
"How can we tell how many there are?"

"What do we call this mark I put at the end of this sentence?"
"Do we have any words that begin with the same letters?"
"Which is the longest word?"

These and similar questions help children learn print tracking and jargon and focus their attention on words and letters.

Include Interactive Writing

Interactive writing is described by Pinnell and Fountas (1998) as "sharing the pen." This notion of not only letting children tell you what to write but letting them "share the pen" is what makes interactive writing different from watching the teacher write and what makes it important to include as another writing format.

To do interactive writing, you gather the children up close to you at a chart or the board, and with the children you think of something you want to write. For beginning lessons, what you write should be quite short—no more than a sentence or two. Perhaps you and the children decide that you should write about Brad's birthday and that the sentences should say:

Today is Brad's birthday. He is six years old.

You then might ask children to look around the room and see if they can find the word "today" anywhere. When a child finds the word, that child is given the pen and comes up and writes *Today*—the first word in the sentence.

The writing continues as the teacher asks if anyone can come up and write *is*. Brad comes and writes his name. The teacher adds the apostrophe and Brad adds the *s*. Together the teacher and children stretch out *birthday*. Different children come and write the letters they can hear, and the teacher fills in the other letters to get *birthday* spelled correctly. Another child volunteers to come and put the period to show that the first sentence is finished.

The same procedure is continued with the second sentence. Children who can spell *he* and *is* come and write those words. *Six* is found on the number chart, and someone comes and writes *six*. *Years* and *old* are stretched out, with volunteers writing letters they can hear and the teacher filling in missing letters. Finally, a child adds the period at the end of the second sentence.

Children love "sharing the pen," and they pay much more attention to the writing when they are a part of it. Regular, short interactive writing sessions should be a part of every young child's day. Lots more detail and examples of more complex lessons can be found in *Word Matters* by Gay Su Pinnell and Irene Fountas.

Children develop crucial understandings as they write, copying some words displayed in the room and stretching out other words to put down sounds they hear.

Let Them Write and Accept Whatever Kind of Writing They Do

Accepting a variety of writing—from scribbling to one-letter representations, to invented spellings, to copied words—is the key to having young children write before they can write. Sometimes, it is the children and not the teacher who reject beginning attempts. If more advanced children give the less advanced children a hard time about their "scribbling," the teacher must intervene and firmly state a policy, such as:

> "There are many different ways to communicate through writing. We use pictures and letters and words. Sometimes we just scribble, but the scribbling

helps us remember what we are thinking. We use all these different ways in this classroom!"

Without this attitude of acceptance, the very children who most need to explore language through writing will be afraid to write.

How Writing Develops Crucial Understandings

Encouraging young children to write has many benefits. As children write, they learn the print concepts of left to right and leaving spaces between words. (Even when children are scribbling, they usually scribble from left to write and stop occasionally to write a new scribble.) Children often write about themselves and each other and copy names of favorite foods, restaurants, and places from the print in the classroom. From these writing opportunities, they learn concrete, important-to-them words. As they stretch out words to "put down the sounds they hear," they are developing phonemic awareness. We are all more apt to remember things we actually use. As children use what they are learning about letters and sounds to try to spell words, they are applying their phonics knowledge. Writing is perhaps our best opportunity for developing young children's print concepts, concrete words, phonemic awareness, and knowledge of letters and sounds. Because they are writing what they want to tell, they also become perfectly clear about what reading and writing are for.

Writing is perhaps the most multilevel activity you can do with young children. Less advanced children begin to develop crucial understandings. More advanced children, who can already write a little, become very fluent writers, delighting teachers and parents.

GETTING TO KNOW YOU

Most teachers begin their year with some get-acquainted activities. As part of these get-acquainted activities, they often have a special child each day. In addition to learning about each child, you can focus attention on the special child's name and use the name to develop some important understandings about words and letters.

To prepare for this activity, write all the children's first names (with initials for last names if two names are the same) with a permanent marker on sentence strips. Cut the strips so that long names have long strips and short names have short strips. Let the children watch you write their names and have them help you spell their names if they can. After writing each name, display it in a pocket chart or other board. As you put each name up, comment on letters shared by certain children or other common features:

"Rasheed's name starts with an *r* just like Robert's."

"Bo's name only takes two letters to write. He has the shortest name but he is one of the tallest boys."

"We have two Ashleys, so I will have to put the first letter of her last name—M—so that we will know which Ashley this is."

We want the children to watch and think as the names are being written, and they usually will because they are so egocentric—interested in themselves—and interested in each other. Their attention for anything, however, diminishes after 15 to 20 minutes, so if you have a large class, you may want to write the names in two different sessions.

Once you have all the names written and displayed, ask volunteers to come and find a name they can read. Many children will read their own and almost everyone will remember *Bo*.

Tell the children that each day one of them will be the special child, and that in order to make it fair—since some children will have to wait 20 or more days—you are going to put all the names in a box, shake up the box, and without looking, draw one of the names. Tell the children what the special child will get to do each day. Some teachers crown that child king or queen, let them lead the line, decide what game to play for P. E., sit in a special chair to greet visitors, pass things out, or take messages to the office. Do keep in mind that whatever you do for the first, you must do for all the rest, so make sure you can sustain whatever you start. (Remember the "Don't do anything the first month of marriage you don't want to do the whole rest of your married life" advice most of us got but ignored.) Each day, reach into the box and draw out a name. This child becomes the special child and the focus of many literacy activities. For our example, we will assume that David is the first name pulled from the box.

Interviewing and Shared Writing

Have David come up and sit in a special chair. Appoint the rest of the class reporters. Their job is to interview David and find out what he likes to eat, play, and do after school. Does he have brothers? Sisters? Cats? Dogs? Mice? Decide on a certain number of questions (5–7) and call on different children to ask the questions.

After the interview, write your "newspaper article" on this special child, using a shared writing format in which the children give suggestions and

Here are some of the charts about the special people in this classroom.

you and they decide what to say first, second, etc. Record this on a chart while the children watch. The chart should not be more than 5–6 sentences long, and the sentences should not be too complex because these articles about each VIP will form some of the first material most children will be able to read. The interview and the writing of the chart should be completed in the 20-minute attention span, and can be if the teacher limits the number of questions and takes the lead in writing the article. This first activity for each child—interviewing and shared writing of the article—develops crucial oral language skills and helps children see how writing and reading occur.

Shared Reading of the Charts

The second activity is the reading of David's chart. This takes place later in the day and, again, does not take more than 20 minutes. On the first day, you will only have one chart to read. Lead the children to read it chorally several times, and let volunteers come and read each sentence. Guide their hands so that they are tracking print as they read. Most teachers display each chart for five days and then let the child take the chart home, with instructions to display it on the child's bedroom door. That way, there are only five charts in the room at any one time, but every chart gets read and reread on five different days.

Many teachers also write (or type) the article from the chart and, after all the children have had their special days and been interviewed, compile a class book containing each article (often along with a picture of each child). Each child then has one night to take the book home so that the family can get to know the whole class.

Focusing on the Name

Now focus everyone's attention on the child's name. Point to the word *David* on the sentence strip and develop children's understanding of jargon by pointing out that this word is David's name. Tell them that it takes many letters to write the word *David*, and let them help you count the letters. Say the letters in *David*, D-a-v-i-d, and have the children chant them with you, cheerleader style. (We call this cheering for David and he loves it!) Point out that the word David begins and ends with the same letter. Explain that the *d* looks different because one is a capital *D* and the other is a small *d*—or uppercase and lowercase—whatever jargon you use.

Take another sentence strip and have children watch as you write *David*. Have them chant the spelling of the letters with you. Cut the letters apart and mix them up. Let several children come and arrange the letters in just the right order so that they spell *David*. Have the other children chant to check that the order is correct. Display David's name on a bulletin board reserved for the names. Many teachers include a photo of each child on this board.

Imagine that on the next day, the name pulled from the box was Catherine. She has been interviewed and a chart article written. Choral and individual readings of her chart along with David's chart have been done. It is now time to focus attention on Catherine's name. Say the letters in *Catherine* and have the children chant them by cheering for Catherine. Help the children to count the letters and decide which letter is first, last, etc. Point out that *Catherine* has two *e*'s and they look exactly the same because they are both small (lowercase) *e*'s. Write *Catherine* on another sentence strip and cut it into letters. Have children arrange the letters to spell *Catherine*, using the first sentence strip name as their model.

Put *Catherine* on the bulletin board and compare the two names. Which has the most letters? How many more letters are in the word *Catherine* than in the word *David*? Does *Catherine* have any of the same letters as *David*?

The next name to come out is *Robert*. Do all the usual activities—interviewing; chart writing; reading of Robert's, Catherine's, and David's charts; cheering for Robert by chanting the letters in his name; writing his name again, cutting it into letters and rearranging the letters to spell his name. Be sure to note the two *r's* and talk about why they look different.

As you put *Robert* on the board or word wall, compare it to *David* and *Catherine*. *Robert* has an *e* and *Catherine* has two *e's*. *Robert* and *Catherine* both have a *t*. *Robert* doesn't have any of the same letters that *David* has. *Robert's* name has six letters—more than *David* but less than *Catherine*.

Mike comes out next. When you have a one-syllable name with which there are many rhymes (*Pat, Tran, Joe, Sue*), seize the opportunity to help the children listen for words that rhyme with that name. Say pairs of words, some of which rhyme with Mike:

Mike/ball;   Mike/bike;   Mike/hike;   Mike/cook;   Mike/like

If the pairs rhyme, everyone should point at Mike and whisper "Mike." If not, they should shake their heads and frown.

Cindy comes out. *Catherine* and *Cindy* both begin with the letter *c* but begin with different sounds. Have Catherine and Cindy stand on opposite sides of you. Write their names above them on the chalkboard. Have the children say *Catherine* and *Cindy* several times, drawing out the first sound. Help them to understand that some letters can have more than one sound and that the names *Catherine* and *Cindy* show us that. Tell the class that you are going to say some words, all of which begin with the letter *c*. Some of these words sound like *Catherine* at the beginning, and some of them sound like *Cindy*. Say some words and have the children say them with you:

cat, celery, candy, cookies, city, cereal, cut

For each word, have them point to Catherine or Cindy to show which sound they hear. Once they have decided, write each word under *Catherine* or *Cindy*.

Continue to pull names each day, and as you add each to your board or wall, help the children notice whatever they can about letter-sound relationships. The names your children have will determine what you will help the children to notice. If you don't have names such as Catherine and Cindy, you would not point out the two sounds of *c* this early in the year, but if you do, you have to help the children understand that some letters have more than one sound or they will get confused. Children do notice things we don't point out, and if we just teach *c* as having the sound in *Catherine, cat,* and *candy,* Cindy may be looking at her nametag and wondering why she can't hear the sound. English is not a one-letter, one-sound language. There are relationships, but they are complex. We must help children see how letters represent sounds, but if we make it simpler than it really is, some children are apt to notice the contradiction and get confused and maybe come to the dangerous conclusion that "there isn't any system and pattern to these letters and sounds."

So if you have a *Joseph* and a *Julio* or a *Sheila* and a *Sam*, use the above procedure when the second name goes up. Point out that it is the *sh* in *Sheila* that gives *s* its different sound. Most of the children who are just beginning to learn about how letters and sounds are related would not need to know this. But those who were already reading when they came to school probably know the single letter sounds and are ready to realize that some letter combinations have different sounds.

Finally, as you get to about the halfway point in adding the names, let the children take charge of noticing the similarities and differences between the names. Instead of pointing out as you add *Rasheed* that his name starts with the same letter and sound as *Robert* and he has two *e*'s and his name ends with a *d* like *David*, ask the children:

> "What do you notice about the letters and sounds in Rasheed's name and the other names on the board?"

There is a system and a pattern to the way letters in English represent sounds. Our instruction should point out these patterns. Children who see a new word and ask themselves how that new word is like the other words they know can discover many patterns on their own.

Writing the Names

The final activity we do with each name is giving the children an opportunity to focus on the name by writing it. (Notice that we are using all the learning modes with each name. They look—visual; they chant—auditory; they write—kinesthetic.) We give each child a sheet of drawing paper and have them write the name in large letters on one side of the paper. We model at the board how to write each letter as they write it, but we do not expect their writing to look just like ours, and we resist the temptation to correct what they wrote. Early in the year, children who haven't written much will reverse letters and make them in funny ways. The important understanding is that names are words, that words can be written, and that it takes lots of letters to write them. We are giving them a kinesthetic way to focus on the word, and although we model correct handwriting, we do not, at this point, expect correct letter formation from everyone.

After they write the name—in whatever fashion they can—have them turn the paper over and draw a picture of that child on the other side of the drawing paper. Let the special child of the day take all the pictures home.

As the learning of each name progresses, some teachers suggest that the children can write just the name or, if they choose to, write one of the

chart sentences or one of their own sentences about the child of the day before turning their paper over to draw. Children who come to school with
more writing ability often enjoy copying one of the chart sentences or making up one of their own, and other children enjoy trying to write the name
and drawing the picture.

Use Names to Build Phonemic Awareness

Phonemic awareness is not just another word for phonics. Phonemic
awareness is the ability to take words apart, put them back together
again, and change them. Phonemic awareness activities are done orally,
calling attention to the sounds—not the letters or which letter makes
which sound.

Clap Syllables   The first way that children learn to pull apart words is into
syllables. Say each child's name and have the children clap the "beats" in
that name as they say it with you. Help children to see that Tran and Pat are
one-beat names, Manuel and Patrick, two beats, and so on. Once children
begin to understand, clap the beats and have all the children whose names
have that number of beats stand up and say their names as they clap the
beats with you.

Matching Beginning Sounds   Say a sound—not a letter name—and have all
the children whose names begin with that sound come forward. Stretch out
the sound as you make it: "s-s-s-s." For the "s-s-s" sound, Samantha, Susie,
Steve, and Cynthia should all come forward. Have everyone stretch out the
"s-s-s" as they say the names. If anyone points out that Cynthia starts with
a *c* or that Sharon starts with an *s*, explain that they are correct about the letters but that now you are listening for sounds.

Hear Rhyming Words   Choose the children whose names have lots of rhyming
words to come forward. Say a word that rhymes with one of the names and
have the children say the word along with the name of the rhyming child.

Segment Words Into Sounds   Call children to line up by stretching out
their names, emphasizing each letter. As each child lines up, have the class
stretch out the name with you.

Use Names to Build Letter-Sound Connections

Of course, we pointed out some letter-sound associations as we did different names, added them to our name board, and asked children what
they noticed. Now that all the names are displayed, however, and most
children have learned most of the names, we can begin to solidify some of

that letter-name sound knowledge. Imagine that the names of our children displayed on the word wall or name board are:

David	Rasheed	Robert	Catherine	Cindy
Mike	Sheila	Sam	Joseph	Julio
Amber T.	Matt	Erin	Shawonda	Bianca
Erica	Kevin	Adam	Delano	Brittany
Bo	Tara	Amber M.	Octavius	Kelsie

Begin with a letter that many children have in their names and that usually has its expected sound. With this class, you might begin with the letter *r*. Have all children whose names have an *r* in them come to the front of the class, each child holding a card with his or her name on it. First count all the *r*'s. There are nine *r*'s in all. Next have the children whose name contains an *r* divide themselves into those whose names begin with an *r* (Robert and Rasheed), those whose names end with an *r* (Amber T. and Amber M.), those with an *r* that is not the first or the last letter (Brittany, Erica, Tara, Erin, Catherine). Finally, say each name slowly, stretching out the letters, and decide if you can hear the usual sound of that letter. For *r*, you can hear the usual sound in all of the names.

Now choose another letter and let all those children come to the front of the class and display their name cards. Count the number of times that letter occurs, and then have the children divide themselves into groups according to whether the letter is first, last, or in between. Finally, say the names, stretching them out, and decide if you can hear the usual sound that letter makes. *D* would be a good second choice. You would have David and Delano beginning with *d*; David and Rasheed ending with *d*; Cindy, Shawonda, and Adam have a *d* that is not first or last. Again, you can hear the usual sound of *d* in all these names.

Continue picking letters and having children come up with their name cards until you have sorted for some of the letters represented by your names. When doing the letters *s*, *c*, *t*, and *j*, be sure to point out that they can have two sounds and that the *th* in *Catherine* and the *sh* in *Sheila*, *Shawonda*, and *Rasheed* have their own special sounds. You probably wouldn't sort out the names with an *h* because although *Shawanda*, *Sheila*, *Rasheed*, *Catherine*, and *Joseph* have an *h*, the *h* sound is not represented by any of these. The same would go for the *p*, which only occurs in *Joseph*. When you have the children come down for the vowels, *a*, *e*, *i*, *o*, and *u*, count and then sort the children according to first, last, and in between, but do not try to listen for the sounds. Explain that vowels have lots of different sounds and that they will learn more about the vowels and their sounds all year.

How Getting to Know You Develops Crucial Understandings

Getting to Know You is a multilevel activity in which there are multiple things to be learned and multiple ways for children to move forward. After participating in the interviewing, shared writing, name board activities, and writing of each child's name, children who enter with almost no understanding of what reading and writing are and how they work are able to:

Track print, starting at the right, pointing to one word at a time, and making the return sweep to the left.

Point to just one word and just one letter, to the first word in a sentence and the first letter in a word, showing they have learned important print jargon and concepts.

Read at least five—and usually many more—of the names of their classmates.

Write many of the names in a fashion that can be read by others. (Even though handwriting may leave much to be desired.)

Name some of the letters of the alphabet.

Demonstrate some understanding that letters and sounds are related by telling you some words—names—that begin with different letters.

In classroom after classroom, children who enter school naive about literacy and who participate in the daily Getting to Know You activities develop those abilities and concepts essential for success in learning to read. More important for the long haul, these children all see themselves as readers and writers and maintain their "Of course I can" attitude.

While these children are developing the critical foundation for moving into literacy, other children who come prepared but not reading are actually learning to read and write. These children can read and write the names of almost all their classmates. They can name all the letters that occur in these names and have begun looking for patterns and relationships between letters and sounds. All of these children can read the chart articles about themselves, and most can read a lot of the words in the articles about the whole class. Most of the children have learned to read many high-frequency words (*the*, *in*, *he*, *she*, *boy*, *girl*, *likes*) that occur over and over in the chart articles. Most can write a sentence about one of their friends.

Finally, we must not forget the children who come already reading. What do they learn through the Getting to Know You activities? These fast learners, as we should expect, make the most progress. They can read fluently all the chart articles, and they can write a several-sentence article about a classmate. Not only can they read words such as *the*, *in*, *he*, *she*, *boy*, *girl*, *likes*, but they have learned to spell them. They have also moved forward in their understanding of how English spelling works. They know that letters can have a variety of sounds, depending on what letters follow them, and they are learning on their own patterns not yet taught because they are used to looking at new words and trying to figure out why the letters do what they do.

Getting to Know You is a truly multilevel activity. Its use accomplishes the goals of moving all levels of children forward and maintaining their enthusiasm and confidence.

LETTER NAMES AND SOUNDS ACTIVITIES

Shared reading, predictable charts, writing, and Getting to Know You are all activities through which children learn many letter names and sounds. There are, however, other activities which children enjoy and which contribute to the development of their letter and sound knowledge.

Singing *The Alphabet Song* and Sharing Alphabet Books

The Alphabet Song (sung to the tune of *Twinkle, Twinkle, Little Star*) has been sung by generations of children. Children enjoy it, and it does seem to give them a sense of all the letters and a framework in which to put new letters as they learn them. Many children come to school already able to sing *The Alphabet Song*. Let them sing it and teach it to everyone else. Once the children can sing the song, you may want to point to alphabet cards (usually found above the chalkboard) as they sing. Children enjoy "being the alphabet" as they line up to go somewhere. Simply pass out laminated alphabet cards—one to each child, leftovers to the teacher—and let the children sing the song slowly as each child lines up. Be sure to hand out the cards randomly so that no one gets to be the *A* and lead the line or has to be the *Z* and bring up the rear every day!

There are also lots of wonderful alphabet books to read and enjoy. Many of these fit into your themes or units. Research shows that the simple books with not too many words on a page and pictures that most of the children recognize are the most helpful to children in building their letter-sound and letter-name knowledge. Once the book has been read and reread several times, children will enjoy reading it during their self-selected reading time. It is very important that children have time to choose and read books each day. Simple alphabet books that have been read together provide books that children can read on their own before they can read books with more text.

There are too many wonderful alphabet books to name them all here, but a few just have to be mentioned. *The Peek-a-Boo ABC* has little doors that you open. Inside the door to the barn is a bear. A clown appears as you open the door to the car, and lions can be found in the lunchbox. When reading this one with children for the second or third time, we pause before opening each door to see if they remember that it is salami in the sandwich and a watermelon in the whale. Another novel alphabet book the children adore is the *A to Z Sticker Book.* Each page has three or four pictures along with the words, and one word with no picture. On the *d* page, you see the words *donkey, dinosaur,* and *dolphins* along with pictures of these. The word *drum* has a space next to it, and you have to find the sticker on the sticker pages in the middle to go with it. Stickers peel off and go back to their spots when the book is read so that the whole process can be done again and again.

Alphabet Books

Here are a few alphabet books that meet our "not too many words, familiar pictures, kids love to read them" criteria:

The Peek-a-Boo ABC (Demi, Random House, 1982)
A to Z Sticker Book (Jan Pienkowski, Random House, 1995)
It Begins with an A. (Stephanie Calmenson, Hyperion, 1993)
Alphabet Puzzle (Jill Downie, Lothrop, 1988)
Dr. Seuss's ABC (Dr. Seuss, Random House, 1963)
The Alphabet Tale (Jan Garten, Random House, 1964)
Easy as Pie (Marcia and Michael Folsom, Houghton Mifflin, 1986)
Eating the Alphabet (Lois Ehlert, Harcourt, 1989)
By the Sea: An Alphabet Book (Ann Blades, Kids Can Press, 1985)
The Accidental Zucchini (Max Grover, Harcourt, 1993)
NBA Action from A to Z (James Preller, Scholastic, 1997)
The Timbertoes ABC Alphabet Book (Highlights for Children, Boyds Mill Press, 1997)
A Is for Astronaut (Stan Tucker, Simon & Schuster, 1995)
Paddington's ABC (Michael Bond, Puffin Books, 1996)
John Burmingham's ABC (John Burmingham, Crown, 1993)
Alphababies (Kim Golding, DK Publishing, 1998)
The Monster Book of ABC Sounds (Alan Snow, Puffin, 1994)

Once you and the children have read several alphabet books, you might want to make a class alphabet book and/or have each child make one. Work on a few pages each day and use all your resources—alphabet books you read to them, things in the room, places children like to eat—to brainstorm a huge list of the possible words for each page. Depending on your class, you may want to put just one word and picture on each page or several words and pictures for each letter. If children are making individual books, let them choose the order in which they will select the letters for the books as well as the words for their pages. They will most often choose the letters they know best first. Knowing that information can help teachers identify what it is that children know.

Letter Actions and Foods

Eating and Actions are important activities to young children. Teaching children actions for the consonant letters and having them associate these letters with foods help some children remember their sounds. For each action, write the letter on one side of a large index card and the action on the other. The first time you teach each letter, make a big deal of it. Get out the rhythm sticks and the marching music when you march. Go out on the playground and jump rope and do jumping jacks. Play hopscotch and pretend to be bunnies when you introduce *h*.

Once the children have learned actions for several letters, there are many activities you can do right in the classroom without any props. Have all the children stand by their desks and wait until you show them a letter. They should do that action until you hide that letter behind your back. When they have all stopped and you have their attention again, show them another letter and have them do that action. Continue this with as many letters as you have time to fill. Be sure to make comments, such as, "Yes, I see everyone marching because *M* is our marching letter."

In another activity, you pass out the letters for which children have learned actions to individual children. Each child gets up and does the action required and calls on someone to guess which letter that child was given.

In "Follow the Letter Leader," the leader picks a letter card and does that action. Everyone else follows the leader doing the same action. The leader then picks another card, and the game continues.

Teachers have different favorite actions, and you will have your own favorites. Try to pick actions with which everyone is familiar and which are called by only one name. Here is a list of actions I like. The action for *s* is my particular favorite. You can use it to end the game. Children say, "It is not an action at all," but they remember that "*s* is the sitting letter":

bounce	hop	nod	vacuum
catch	jump	paint	walk
dance	kick	run	yawn
fall	laugh	sit	zip
gallop	march	talk	

This class has made an alphabet mural, which they are about to hang in the hall.

Children remember what they do and what they eat. Many teachers like to feature a food when they are studying a particular letter. Children help to prepare the food and then eat it. Try to pick nutritious foods which children like, although even the children who hated zucchini remembered it was their z food! When they complained, their teacher asked, "What food do you like that begins with z?" Later, a child brought zucchini bread, which was a hit with most. Some possible foods:

bananas	hamburgers	noodles	vegetables
cookies	Jello	pizza	watermelon
donuts	Kool-Aid	raisins	yogurt
fish	lemonade	soup	zucchini bread
gum	milk	toast	

PHONEMIC AWARENESS

Many of the activities discussed previously in this chapter help children develop phonemic awareness. As they participate in shared reading and writing, they become aware of words as separate entities. Being the Words, cutting sentences into words and rearranging them, making new sentences from familiar words—all help children understand what words are. Encouraging invented spelling is one of the main ways teachers have of helping children develop their understanding of how phonemes make up words. As children try to spell words, they say them slowly, listening to themselves saying the sounds and thinking about what they are learning about letters and sounds. Following are other activities you can use to promote phonemic awareness.

Count Words

To count words, all children should have 10 counters in a paper cup. (Anything manipulable is fine. Some teachers use edibles such as raisins, grapes, or small crackers and let the children eat their counters at the end of the lesson. This makes clean-up quick and easy.) Begin by counting some familiar objects in the room (windows, doors, trash cans), having all children place one of their counters on their desks as each object is pointed to. Have children return counters to the cup before beginning to count the next object.

Tell children that you can also count words by putting down a counter for each word you say. Explain that you will say a sentence in the normal way and then repeat the sentence, pausing after each word. The children should put down counters as you slowly say the words in the sentence, and then count the counters and decide how many words you said. As usual, children's attention is better if you make sentences about them. (Carol has a big smile. Paul is back at school today. I saw Jack at the grocery store.) Once the children catch on to the activity, let them say some sentences, first in the normal way, then one word at a time. Listen carefully as they say their sentences the first time because they will often need help saying them one word at a time. Children enjoy this activity, and not only are they learning to separate out words in speech, they are also practicing critical counting skills.

Clap Syllables

Once children can automatically separate the speech stream into words, they are ready to begin thinking about separating words into some components. The first division most children learn to make is that of syllables. Clapping seems the easiest way to get every child involved, and the children's names (what else?) are the naturally appealing words to clap. Say the first name of one child. Say the name again, and this time, clap the syllables. Continue saying first names and then clapping the syllables as you say them the second time, and invite the children to join in clapping with you. As children catch on, say some middle or last names. The term *syllables* is a little jargony and foreign to most young children, so you may want to refer to the syllables as beats. Children should realize by clapping that *Paul* is a one-beat word, *Miguel* is a two-beat word, and *Madeira* is a three-beat word.

Once children can clap syllables and decide how many beats a given word has, help them to see that one-beat words are usually shorter than three-beat words—that is, they take fewer letters to write. To do this, write on sentence strips some words children cannot read, and cut the strips into words so that short words have short strips and long words have long strips. Have some of the words begin with the same letters but be different lengths so that children will need to think about word length to decide which word is which.

For the category *animals,* you might write horse and hippopotamus; dog and donkey; kid and kangaroo; and rat, rabbit, and rhinoceros. Tell the children that you are going to say the names of animals and they should clap to show how many beats the word has. (Do not show them the words yet!) Say the first pair, one at a time (horse, hippopotamus) and have the children say them. Help children to decide that horse is a one-beat word and hippopotamus takes a lot more claps and is a five-beat word. Now, show them the two words and say, "One of these words is horse and the other is hippopotamus. Who thinks they can figure out which one is horse and which one is hippopotamus?" Help the children by explaining that because hippopotamus takes so many beats to say it, it probably takes more letters to write it. Continue with other pairs—and finally with a triplet—rat, rabbit, rhinocerous—to make it more multilevel.

Do Nursery Rhymes

One of the best indicators of how well children will learn to read is their ability to recite nursery rhymes when they walk into the kindergarten. Since this is such a reliable indicator, and since rhymes are so naturally appealing to children at this age, kindergarten classrooms should be filled with rhymes. Children should learn to recite these rhymes, sing the rhymes, clap to the rhymes, act out the rhymes, and pantomime the rhymes. In some kindergarten classrooms, they develop "raps" for the rhymes.

Once the children can recite many rhymes, nursery rhymes can be used to teach the concept of rhyme. The class can be divided into two halves—one half says the rhyme but stops when they get to the last rhyming word. The other half waits to shout the rhyme at the appropriate moment:

First half:	There was an old woman who lived in a shoe. She had so many children, she didn't know what to
Second half:	do.
First half:	She gave them some broth without any bread, and spanked them all soundly and put them to
Second half:	bed.

Nursery and other rhymes have been a part of our oral heritage for generations. Now we know that the rhythm and rhyme inherent in nursery rhymes are important vehicles for the beginning development of phonemic awareness. They should play a large role in any kindergarten curriculum.

Do Rhymes and Riddles

Young children are terribly egocentric, and they are very "body oriented." In doing rhymes and riddles, therefore, have children point to different body parts to show rhyming words. Tell children that you are going to say some words that rhyme with *head* or *feet*. After you say each word, have the children repeat the word with you and decide if the word rhymes with *head* or *feet*. If the word you say rhymes with *head*, they should point to their head. If it rhymes with *feet*, they should point to their feet. As children point, be sure to respond, acknowledging a correct response by saying something like, "Carl is pointing to his head because *bread* rhymes with *head*." You may want to use some of these words:

meet	bread	led	sleet
seat	red	sheet	fed
bed	beat	sled	thread
dead	greet	heat	shed

Now, ask the children to say the missing word in the following riddles (the answers all rhyme with *head*):

On a sandwich, we put something in between the ...
When something is not living anymore, it is ...
To sew, you need a needle and ...
The color of blood is ...
We can ride down snowy hills on a ...

Here are other riddles, the answers to which rhyme with *feet*:

Steak and pork chops are different kinds of ...
On a crowded bus, it is hard to get a ...
You make your bed with a ...
When you are cold, you turn on the ...

If children like this activity, do it again, but this time have them listen for words that rhyme with *hand* or *knee*. If the word you say rhymes with *hand*, they should point to their hand. If it rhymes with *knee*, they should point to their knee. Some words to use are:

sand	band
land	see
me	bee
stand	grand
we	free
brand	tea
tree	and

Here are some riddles for *hand*:

At the beach, you dig in the ...
To build a house, you must first buy a piece of ...
The musicians who march and play in a parade are called a ...
You can sit or you can ...

And some more which rhyme with *knee*:

You use your eyes to ...
You could get stung by a ...
If something doesn't cost anything, we say it is ...
You can climb up into a ...

To challenge your class, have them make up riddles and point for words that rhyme with *feet, knee, hand,* or *head.* As each child gives a riddle, have the riddle giver point to the body part that rhymes with the answer. Model this for the children by doing a few to show them how.

Sing Rhymes and Read Lots of Rhyming Books

Many children come to school with well-developed phonemic awareness abilities, and these children usually come from homes in which rhyming chants, jingles, and songs were part of their daily experience. These same chants, jingles, and songs should be a part of every young child's day in the classroom.

There are many wonderful rhyming books, but because of their potential to develop phonemic awareness, two deserve special mention. Along with other great rhyming books, Dr. Seuss wrote *There's a Wocket in My Pocket*. In this book, all kinds of Seussian creatures are found in various places. In addition to the wocket in the pocket, there is a vug under the rug, a nureau in the bureau, and a yottle in the bottle! After several readings, children delight in chiming in to provide the nonsensical word and scary creature that lurks in harmless-looking places. After reading the book a few times, it is fun to decide what creatures might be lurking in your classroom. Let children make up the creatures, and accept whatever they say as long as it rhymes with their object:

"There's a pock on our clock!"

"There's a zindow looking in our window!"

"There's a zencil on my pencil!"

Another wonderful rhyming book for phonemic awareness is *The Hungry Thing* by Jan Slepian and Ann Seidler. In this book, a large friendly dinosaur-looking creature (You have to see him to love him!) comes to town, wearing a sign that says,

"Feed Me."

When asked what he would like to eat, he responds,

"Shmancakes."

After much deliberation, a clever little boy offers him some pancakes. The Hungry Thing eats them all up and demands,

"Tickles."

Again, after much deliberation, the boy figures out he wants pickles. As the story continues, it becomes obvious that The Hungry Thing wants specific foods and that he asks for them by making them rhyme with what he wants.

He asks for *feetloaf* and gobbles down the meatloaf. For dessert, he wants *hookies* and *gollipops*.

The Hungry Thing is a delightful book, and in many classrooms, teachers have made a poster-size Hungry Thing, complete with his sign that reads "Feed Me" on one side and "Thank You!" on the other. Armed with real foods or pictures of foods, the children try to feed The Hungry Thing. Of course, he won't eat the food unless they make it rhyme. If they offer him spaghetti, they have to say,

"Want some bagetti?" (or zagetti, or ragetti—any silly word that rhymes with spaghetti).

To feed him *Cheerios*, they have to offer him *seerios*, *theerios*, or *leerios*.

Once you have found some wonderful books with lots of rhymes, follow these steps to assure your children are learning to recognize and produce rhymes:

1. Pick a book with lots of rhyme that you think your children will "fall in love with." Read, enjoy, and talk about the content of the book, and let children become thoroughly comfortable and familiar with the book. Remember that children who are lucky enough to own books want books read to them again and again.

This boy is trying to feed a pumpkin to the hungry thing. "Hungry Thing, would you like to eat a **bumpkin**?"

2. Once the children are very familiar with the book, reread it again, and tell them that the author of this book made it "fun to say" by including lots of rhymes. Read the book, stopping after each rhyme, and have children identify the rhyming words and say them with you.

3. For the next reading, tell children that you are going to stop and have them fill in the rhyming word. Read the whole book, stopping each time and having children supply the rhyming word.

4. The activities in steps 2 and 3 have helped children identify rhymes. We also want children to produce rhymes. Depending on the book, find a way to have children make up similar rhymes. Producing rhymes was what children were doing when they made up rhyming items "the zencil on the pencil" and tried to feed new things like "theerios" to The Hungry Thing.

Recognizing and producing rhymes is one of the critical components of phonemic awareness. Children who engage in these kinds of activities with wonderful rhyming books will develop the concept of rhyme.

Play Blending and Segmenting Games

In addition to hearing and producing rhyme, the ability to put sounds together to make a word—blending—and the ability to separate out the sounds in a word—segmenting—are critical components of phonemic

---

There are lots of wonderful rhyming books that can be used to develop phonemic awareness. A few of our favorites are:

Any rhyming book by Dr. Seuss
There's a Wocket in My Pocket (Dr. Seuss, Random House, 1974)
The Hungry Thing (Jan Slepian and Ann Seidler, Scholastic, 1988)
"I Can't," Said the Ant (Polly Cameron, Coward, 1961)
Jake Baked the Cake (B. G. Hennessey, Viking, 1990)
Pretend You're a Cat (Jean Marzollo, Dial, 1990)
Ape in a Cape (Fritz Eichenberg, Harcourt, 1952)
Catch a Little Fox (Beatrice De Regniers, Scholastic, 1968)
Buzz Said the Bee (Wendy Lewison, Scholastic, 1992)
Moose on the Loose (Carol Ochs, Carolrhoda, 1991)
Down by the Bay (Raffi, Crown, 1987)
There's a Bug in My Mug and *My Nose Is a Rose* (Kent Salisbury, McClanahan, 1997)

awareness. Blending and segmenting are not easy for many children. In general, it is easier for them to segment off the beginning letters—the onset—from the rest of the word—the rime—than it is to separate all the sounds. In other words, children can usually separate *bat* into *b-at* before they can produce the three sounds *b-a-t*. The same is true for blending. Most children can blend *S-am* to produce the name *Sam* before they can blend *S-a-m*. Most teachers begin by having children blend and segment the onset from the rime, and then move to blending and segmenting individual letters.

There are lots of games children enjoy that can help them learn to blend and segment. The most versatile is a simple riddle guessing game. The teacher begins the game by naming the category and giving the clue:

"I'm thinking of an animal that lives in the water and is a f-ish." (or f-i-sh, depending on what level of blending you are working on)

The child who correctly guesses "fish" gives the next riddle:

"I'm thinking of an animal that goes quack and is a d-uck." (or d-u-ck)

This sounds simplistic, but children love it, and you can use different categories to go along with units you are studying.

A wonderful variation on this guessing game is to put objects in a bag and let children reach in the bag to choose one. Then they stretch out the name of the object and call on someone to guess "What is it?" Choose small common objects you find in the room—a cap, a ball, chalk, a book. Let the children watch you load the bag and help you stretch out the words for practice as you put them in.

Children also like to talk like "ghosts." One child chooses an object in the room to say as a ghost would, stretching the word out very slowly: "dddoooorrr." The child who correctly guesses "door" gets to ghost talk another object—"bbbooookkk." The ghost-talk game and the guessing game provide practice in segmenting and blending as children segment words by stretching them out and other children blend the words together to guess them.

Tongue Twisters and Books With Lots of Alliteration
In addition to concepts of rhyme, blending, and segmenting, children must learn what it means that words "start the same." This understanding must be in place before children can make sense of the notion that particular letters make particular sounds. Many children confuse the concept of words beginning or starting with the same sound with the

These three practical books give you lots of "fun" activities for helping children develop phonemic awareness:

Fitzpatrick, J. (1997). *Phonemic Awareness: Playing With Sounds to Strengthen Beginning Reading Skills.* Cypress, CA: Creative Teaching Press.

Ericson, L., & Juliebo, M. F. (1998*) The Phonological Awareness Handbook for Kindergarten and Primary Teachers.* Newark, DE: International Reading Association.

Hajdusiewicz, B. B. (1998). *Phonics through Poetry: Teaching Phonemic Awareness Using Poetry.* Glenview, IL: Goodyear.

concept of rhyme, so many teachers like to wait until the concept of rhyme is firmly established for most children before focusing on whether or not words begin with the same sound. Just as for rhyme, we would build a lot of our work with words that start the same by choosing wonderful books such as *All About Arthur—an Absolutely Absurd Ape* by Eric Carle. Arthur, an ape who plays the accordion, travels around the country meeting lots of other musicians—including, in Baltimore, a bear who plays a banjo, and a yak in Yonkers. *Dr. Seuss's ABC,* in which each letter of the alphabet has a sentence such as "Many mumbling mice are making midnight music in the moonlight," is another excellent example of an appealing book that helps children understand what it means to "start the same." In using alliterative books, we would follow the same steps followed with rhyming books:

1. Read and enjoy the book several times.
2. Point out that the author used some "start the same" words to make the book fun to say, and identify these words.
3. Let the children say the "start the same" words with you as you read the book again.
4. Have the children come up with other words that "start the same" that the author could have used on that page.

Once you have read and enjoyed several tongue-twister books, why not create a tongue-twister book for your class? Let the children help you make up the tongue twisters, and add two or three each day. Turn them into posters or bind them into a class book and let the children read them with you several times—as slow as they can and as fast as they can. Help the children understand that what makes tongue twisters hard to say fast is that the words all start the same and you keep having to get your mouth and tongue into the same place. The same first sound repeated over and over is also what makes them so much fun to say. Here are some to get you started. You and your children can surely make up better ones. Be sure to use children's names from your class when they have the right letters and sounds!

> Billy's baby brother bopped Betty.
> Carol can catch caterpillars.
> David dozed during dinner.
> Fred's father fell fifty feet.
> Gorgeous Gloria gets good grades.
> Hungry Harry hates hamburgers.
> Jack juggled Jill's jewelry.
> Kevin's kangaroo kicked Karen.
> Louie likes licking lemon lollipops.
> Mike's mom makes marvelous meatballs.
> Naughty Nellie never napped nicely.
> Patty picked pink pencils.
> Roger Rabbit runs relays.
> Susie's sister sipped seven sodas.
> Tom took ten turtles to town.
> Veronica visited very vicious volcanoes.
> Wild Willy went west.
> Yippy yanked Yolanda's yellow yoyo.
> Zany Zeb zapped Zeke's zebra.

As you work with books with lots of words that begin the same and tongue twisters, begin by emphasizing the words that start the same. This is the phonemic awareness understanding that underlies phonics knowledge. When your children can tell you whether or not words start with the same sound and can come up with other words that start that way, shift your instruction to which letter makes which sound. You can use the very same books and tongue twisters again, this time emphasizing the sound of the letter. Books with alliteration and tongue twisters can help your children develop the "starts the same" component of phonemic awareness and can help them learn some letter sounds.

Tongue-Twister Books

Here are some wonderful tongue-twister books:

Faint Frogs Feeling Feverish and Other Terrifically Tantalizing Tongue Twisters (Obligada, L, 1983)
All About Arthur—an Absolutely Absurd Ape (Eric Carle, 1974)
Dr. Seuss's ABC (Dr. Seuss, Random House 1963)
The Biggest Tongue Twister Book in the World (Gyles Brandeth, Sterling, 1978)
Alphabet Annie Announces an All-American Album (Susan Purviance and Marcia O'shell, Houghton Mifflin, 1988)
A Twister of Twists, A Tangler of Tongues and *Busy Buzzing Bumblebees and Other Tongue Twisters* (Alvin Schwartz, Harper Collins, 1972)
Six Sick Sheep (Jan Cole, Morrow, 1993)
Animalia (Graeme Base, Abrams, 1987)

Sound Boxes

Some children find it very difficult to segment words into sounds. Many teachers have found success using a technique called sound boxes (Elkonin, 1973), in which children push chips, pennies, or other objects into boxes as they hear the sounds. In the first lessons, children have a drawing of three boxes.

The teacher says familiar words composed of three sounds, such as *cat, sun, dog, pan.* Often children are shown pictures of these objects. After naming each object, the teacher and children "stretch out" the three sounds, distorting the word as little as possible: "sssuuunnn." Children push a chip into each box as they say that part of the word. It is important to note here that the boxes represent sounds—phonemes—not letters. *Cake, bike,* and *duck* have three sounds, but four letters. These words would be segmented into three sound boxes. Once children get good at segmenting words with three sounds, they are given a drawing with four boxes and they stretch out some four-phoneme words such as *truck, crash* and *nest*. Sound boxes are used extensively to develop phonemic awareness in children in Reading Recovery™ (Clay, 1985), a highly successful one-on-one tutoring program that works with first graders in the bottom 20 percent of the class.

Once children can push the chips to represent sounds, they can push letter cards into boxes. From the letters *m, b, s, t* and *a*, the teacher could ask the children to push these letters to spell words such as *sat, bat, mat, bam, Sam, tab, bats, mats, tabs,* and *stab*. Children should not work with letters in the sound boxes until they have developed some phonemic awareness and are working on learning letter names and letter sounds. Later on, children can actually write the letters in the boxes as they are attempting to spell words they are writing.

ESTABLISH KEY WORDS FOR SOUNDS

Once your children are moving along in their phonemic awareness, have learned many of the letter names, and are beginning to learn some of the sounds, you can help them consolidate this knowledge by deciding with them on one key word to represent each sound. Many publishing companies and reading series include some key words for the common letter sounds, but often children call the word something other than what is intended ("puppy" for *dog* or "bunny" for *rabbit*, for example), and the key words confuse rather than support their learning of letter sounds. Our suggestion is that you work with your class to come up with a key word that works for you. Let all the children have a say in this, and spend some time discussing which word would be most helpful and which word they like best. Remember that "liking something" is very important to young children! You may want to use some of the wonderful examples from alphabet books, some of the names of your children when they are clear examples for the sound, and some favorite foods and favorite places familiar to all your children. For the vowels, you may want two examples, one for each of the common sounds. Try to use "pure" sounds—a word with just *f*, not *fr* or *fl*—since separating these blended sounds is difficult for children in the beginning. Here are the key words one class decided they liked. The names are all names of children in the class or of famous people. Use this as an example of the kind of chart your children might help construct, but remember this only works if the children have ownership in choosing the words and if they like their choices.

A a	apple, ape		N n	nose
B b	boys		O o	octopus, Oprah
C c	cookies		P p	Pizza Hut
D d	dinosaur		Q u	quarter
E e	elephant, Ethan		R r	red
F f	fun		S s	soup
G g	girls		T t	Taco Bell
H h	Hardees		U u	underwear, unicorn
I i	insect, ice cream		V v	Vicki
J j	Jessica		W w	Wendys
K k	K-mart		X x	x-ray
L l	Latecia		Y y	yellow
M m	McDonalds		Z z	zoo

The series

Alphabet Starters (Rigby, 1996) provides little books for each letter of the alphabet. Each book contains seven key words with wonderfully clear pictures. The *g* book has words and pictures for *gate, girls, goats, garage, garden, goggles,* and *guitar*. The *r* book has *rabbit, red, road, river, rainbow, ring,* and *rope*. Books for the vowels have pictures and words for both the long and short sounds. The *i* book has *insects, invitation, igloo, ice cream,* and an *iron*. Young children love reading these simple but engaging books, and they help them learn letter sounds along with the important phonemic awareness concept of "starts the same."

ASSESSING PROGRESS

Assessment is an ongoing process for experienced teachers who have become good kid watchers. As the children respond to the various activities, teachers notice who can do what. Write down what you notice and you have anecdotal records! Samples—particularly writing samples and audio-taped samples of children reading—are also informative. By comparing samples done across time, growth can be determined and validated. Here are some ideas for ongoing assessment of print concepts, phonemic awareness, concrete words, and letter names and sounds.

Print Concepts

One essential part of the foundation for learning to read is the ability to track print and what we are talking about when we ask them to look at the first word or the last letter or the fact that *Robert* and *Rasheed* begin with the same sound. These print concepts are essential to successfully beginning the journey toward literacy and thus are some of the most important concepts to assess during the first month of school. Many teachers use a checklist that includes:

> Starts on left
> Goes left to right
> Makes return sweep to next line
> Matches words by pointing to each as reading
> Can point to just one word
> Can point to the first word and the last word
> Can point to just one letter
> Can point to the first letter and the last letter

Teachers use the checklist as children are reading in the Big Books or participating in predictable chart activities. As different children volunteer to read, the teacher asks them to point to what they are reading. She also asks them if they can show just one word, point to the first and last word, show just one letter, point to the first and last letters of a word. If they are successful, she puts a plus in the column showing what they have demonstrated. When children have two pluses in a column from two different days, the teacher assumes this child has the concept and doesn't check this anymore for this child. When children demonstrate that they have all these concepts, the teacher draws a line through their name and focuses the instruction and assessment on children who have not yet demonstrated these concepts.

Children who are not successful have minuses put in their columns so that the teacher knows to continue to give them practice and watch their progress. Many teachers work individually or in a small group with children who still have not mastered these concepts by rereading Big Books or charts and focusing them on these concepts.

Phonemic Awareness

Children who have phonemic awareness can manipulate words. They can clap syllables in words and know that the word *motorcycles* takes more claps than the word *car*. They can stretch out words and tell you what word you have said when you stretch one out. They can tell you that *bike* rhymes with *Mike* and that *book* doesn't. After enjoying and participating in *There's a Wocket in My Pocket* activities, they can make up silly rhymes for objects in the classroom. They can get *The Hungry Thing* to eat their food by making up a word that rhymes with what they want to feed it.

We would assess their phonemic awareness by observing their ability to do these rhyming word tasks as we were doing the activities with the whole class. Just as for print concepts, we would require two plusses on two different days before deciding they had developed the concept. Phonemic awareness is not a single concept and is not an easy concept for many children. Not all children will have all parts of it even after several months. Some will need continued nudges toward developing this as we move into more advanced decoding and spelling activities.

Word Learning

Many children enter school with some known words. The words they know are usually "important to them" concrete words. Children who come to school already able to read or write some concrete words have accomplished an important and difficult task. They have learned how to learn words.

All children should have learned some words from the reading, writing, and word activities described in this chapter. To assess their word learning, you may want to check their ability to read the names of the children in the class, some of the most interesting words such as *fox, hen,* and *pig* from a Big Book such as *Hattie and the Fox.* For children who came already knowing some concrete words, you may want to see if they have learned some of the high-frequency words—such as *like, is, in, the*—often repeated in the Big Book and in many of the chart articles. The expectation should not be that anyone is learning all words (although your children who came already reading will astound you with how little repetition they require to learn a word), but that everyone is adding some words to their store of words they can read.

Letter Names and Sounds

We assess their letter name and sound knowledge by showing them a sheet containing all the letters in upper- and lowercase form and asking them to point to any letters they know. Children look over the sheet and find some they know, and we note these on their record sheet with an *n* for *name.* Once they have done this, we point to some of the letters they didn't name and ask:

"Can you tell me what sound this letter makes?"

If they give us an appropriate sound, we indicate this with an *s* for *sound* on their record sheet. Next, we point to some of the letters they haven't identified and ask:

"Do you know any words that begin with this letter?"

We indicate with a *w* for *word* any letters they didn't give us names or sounds for but for which they do have a word association.

Using What You Learn From Assessment

For those children who lack print concepts, have them come up and point to words with you as the rest of the class rereads a page from a Big Book or a chart. Help them to identify the first word and the last word, and to find two words that begin with the same letter. As you are writing a morning message or some other shared writing activity, ask them to come show you where to start and where to put the next word when you have finished one line.

For those children who lack phonemic awareness, be sure that they are saying rhymes, tongue twisters, and other activities with you and the rest of the class, not just listening while others say them. These children might come up and lead the class in repeating favorite chants, for example. After someone else has identified the rhyming words, or words that begin alike, have the child repeat what that child said. "Bo, can you tell me what words Rasheed said rhymed?"

All children should be learning some words—a few very important-to-them words for your struggling children and lots of words for children who came to school with lots of reading and writing experiences. The difference in the number of words learned is to be expected. What you want to monitor is that your struggling children are learning some words.

The same is true for letter names and sounds. Some children need a lot of practice to learn letter names and sounds. What is important is that you know how children are progressing in their learning of some letter names and sounds, and that you continue to provide opportunities for children to associate letter names and sounds with interesting words as long as you have children who still need to build these associations.

This chapter has described a variety of activities used by kindergarten and first-grade teachers who want all children to have the foundation needed to become readers and writers. These activities are also successful with older children who still need to develop the foundation, particularly children learning English. These activities engage the children in reading and writing and help them see how words, letters, and

KINDERGARTEN KIDWATCHING CHECKLIST

Student Name _____	JAN.	MAR.	JUNE
Words—Can recognize			
3 names			
3 days of the week			
3 weather words			
Letter Names—Can recognize			
A D B M S R			
o i e c t n			
Phonemic Awareness			
Can clap the beats for 3 names			
Matches pictures with rhyming words			
Concepts of Print			
Finds the front of a book			
Starts on left side of the page			
Goes left to right across the page			
Makes return sweep to next line			
Matches words by pointing to each word as reading			
Can point to just one word			
Can point to the first word and the last word			
Can point to just one letter			
Can point to the first letter and the last letter of a word			

Comments

Here is the checklist one kindergarten teacher used to assess her children's development of concrete words, letter names, phonemic awareness, and concepts of print.

From *Month-by-Month Reading and Writing for Kindergarten*. (Hall & Cunningham, 1998). Material appears courtesy of Carson-Dellosa Publishing Company, Inc.

sounds are part of reading and writing. The activities include many different response modes and contain a variety of things to be learned from each so that all children can enjoy and learn from them. Jargon is used only as needed, and the concrete thing represented by the jargon is always there so children learn the words they need to communicate about reading and writing.

All the activities are multilevel—they have different things you can learn from them depending on where you are. Children who come ahead will continue to move ahead as children lacking print experiences build the necessary foundation. Finally, the activities are truly activities! The children are active! They are seldom just sitting and listening; they move, sing, chant, act, draw, write, and read.

REFERENCES

Clay, M. M. (1985). *The early detection of reading difficulties* (3rd ed.). Portsmouth, NH: Heinemann.

Elkonin, D. B. (1973). Reading in the USSR. In J. Downing (Ed.), *Comparative reading* (pp. 551–579). New York: Macmillan.

Hall, D. P. & Cunningham, P. M. (1998). *Month by month reading and writing for kindergarten.* Greensboro, NC: Carson-Dellosa.

Hoffman, J., Cunningham, P. M., Cunningham, J. W., & Yopp, H. (1998). *Phonemic awareness and the teaching of reading.* Newark, DE: International Reading Association.

Lundberg, I., Frost, J., & Petersen, O-P. (1988). Effects of an extensive program for stimulating phonological awareness in preschool children. *Reading Research Quarterly, 23,* 264–284.

Pinnell, G. S., & Fountas, I. (1998). *Word matters.* Portsmouth: NH: Heinemann.

Sulzby, E., Teale, W. H., & Kamberelis, G. (1989). Emergent writing in the classroom: Home and school connections. In D. S. Strickland & L. M. Morrow (Eds.), *Emerging literacy: Young children learn to read and write.* Newark, DE: International Reading Association.

Teale, W. H., & Sulzby, E. (1991). Emergent literacy." In R. Barr, M. Kamil, P. Mosenthal, & P. D. Pearson (Eds.), *Handbook of reading research,* Vol. 2. (pp. 418–452). New York: Longman.

CHILDREN'S BOOKS CITED

(In addition to the books listed in boxes on pages 33, 43, 46, and 48, these books are also cited in the chapter.)

Are You My Mother?, by P. D. Eastman (Random House, 1988 [reissue].)

Brown Bear, Brown Bear, What Do You See?, by Bill Martin, Jr. (Henry Holt, 1996 [reissue].)

Goodnight Moon, by Margaret Wise Brown (Scholastic, 1989.)

Hatttie and the Fox, by Mem Fox (Simon and Schuster, 1988.)

Things I Like, by Anthony Browne (Random House, 1989.)

2
READING AND SPELLING
HIGH-FREQUENCY WORDS

One hundred words account for almost half of all the words we read and write (Fry, Fountoukidis, & Polk, 1985). Ten words—*the*, *of*, *and*, *a*, *to*, *in*, *is*, *you*, *that*, and *it*—account for almost one-quarter of all the words we read and write. As soon as possible, children should learn to read and spell these high-frequency words.

When children at an early age learn to recognize and automatically spell the most frequently occurring words, all their attention is freed for decoding and spelling less frequent words and, more important, for processing meaning. Stopping to figure out a new word while reading, or stopping to say the word slowly and figure out how you might spell it while writing, requires time and mental energy. In fact, stopping to think about a new word takes your attention away from meaning. Psychologists explain that we all have limited attention spans, sometimes called short-term memory. Short-term memory is the place that holds words or other bits of information. The short-term memory span for most people is about seven words. When we read, we hold the words in short-term memory until we have enough words to make meaning from them. Meaning can then go into long-term memory. Thus, we make meaning from the words stored in short-term memory and send that meaning to long-term memory. This frees up all our short-term memory space for more words, and the process continues. So it goes, until we need our short-term memory space for something else—like figuring out the pronunciation of a new word. Writing works the same way. We spell most words automatically, and when we have to stop to figure out the spelling of a word, our attention moves from what we are writing to how to spell a particular word.

Decoding or figuring out the spelling of a new word takes all our short-term memory space. In fact, when this decoding process begins, all words already read or written and stored in short-term memory are dumped out (into the garbage disposal, I think). This dumping explains why, once the new word is decoded or spelled, we must quickly reread any prior words in that sentence so that we may put them in short-term memory again. It also explains why children who have to decode many words often don't know what they have read after they read it! Their short-term memory space keeps getting preempted for decoding tasks, and they can't reread every sentence over and over. So they never get enough words in short-term memory from which to make meaning to put in long-term memory. All their attention is required for figuring out words, and there is no capacity for putting together meaning. In order to read and write fluently with comprehension and meaning, children must be able to automatically read and spell the most frequent words. As the store of words they can automatically read and spell increases, so will their speed and comprehension.

The second reason we want children to automatically recognize and spell high-frequency words is that many of the most frequent words are not pronounced or spelled in logical ways: if *the* were pronounced like other words with the same spelling pattern, it would rhyme with *he, me,* and *be; to* would rhyme with *go, no,* and *so; said* would rhyme with *maid* and *paid;* and *have* would rhyme with *cave* and *wave.* If *they, was,* and *come* were spelled logically, they would be spelled the way many children spell them— t-h-a-y, w-u-z, c-u-m.

The apparent lack of logic in how the most frequent words are spelled and pronounced has a logical—and historical—explanation. The way we pronounce words changes with use. The words used most often are, of course, the words whose pronunciation has changed the most. In most cases, pronunciation shifts to an easier pronunciation. It is quicker and easier to get your tongue in position to say "the" in the usual way than it is to make it rhyme with *he, me,* and *we.* "Said" takes longer to say if you make it rhyme with *paid* and *maid.* Children should learn to read and spell the most frequently occurring words because these are the words they will read and write over and over. Many of them cannot be decoded, and if you spell them logically, you will often be wrong.

The problem is that many struggling readers have a great deal of difficulty learning these words. They often know them today and forget them tomorrow. This chapter will focus on strategies that have been successful in teaching everyone—even the children who need multiples practices—to read and spell the most frequent words.

BUILDING MEANING FOR HIGH-FREQUENCY WORDS

The first problem many children have with the high-frequency words is that most of these have no meaning. Unlike *dinosaur*, *apples*, and *happy*, words like *are*, *is*, and *have* are functional, connecting, abstract words children cannot connect any meaning to. How do you explain, demonstrate, or otherwise make sense of words like *of*, *for*, and *from*? In addition, what meaning they do have changes from minute to minute. *There* is the opposite of *here*, but if you move across the room, there becomes here! *This* becomes *that* and *these* become *those*.

In addition to the problems these words create by having no concrete consistent meaning, many of the frequently occurring words share the same letters. Besides the often confused *of*, *for*, and *from* and the reversible words *on/no*, *was/saw*, beginners are always confusing the *th* and the *w* words:

the	there	their	this	that
they	them	then	these	those
what	want	went	when	who
why	were	where	will	with

To many children, remembering these words is like trying to remember the pronunciation of words in a foreign language when you don't know what they mean and they don't follow any standard spelling system. No wonder they know them today and forget them tomorrow.

What kind of activities can we provide to ensure that all children will learn to read and write these critical words? The most important factor to consider in teaching the highly frequent words seems to be the meaning— or, more specifically, the lack of meaning—factor.

In Chapter One, we discussed learning letter names and how children who knew some concrete words that contained the letters remembered the letters better because they had associated the letters with the already-known words. Associative learning is always more permanent than rote learning. Since these frequent words have no meaning in and of themselves, we must help the children associate them with something meaningful. To introduce the word *of*, for example, we might have pictures of a piece of pie, a can of Coke, and a box of cookies. These pictures would be labeled *a piece of pie*, *a can of Coke*, *a box of cookies* with the word *of* underlined. Next, the children would think of other things they like to eat and drink with the word *of*, such as a glass of milk, a bowl of soup, a piece of bubble gum. The labeled pictures would then be displayed to help students associate meaning with this abstract word.

a piece <u>of</u> cake   a box <u>of</u> cookies   a bowl <u>of</u> soup

After an abstract word is associated with meaning, there must be practice with that word. This practice can take many forms; but it should not consist solely of looking at the word and saying it. Not all children are good visual learners. Many children need to do something in order to learn something. Chanting the spelling of words and writing the words provide children with auditory and kinesthetic routes to learning and remembering abstract words.

Once the children can associate meaning with a word such as *of* and have practiced *of* enough times to be able to read it and spell it, it is time to introduce one of the words with which *of* is often confused, such as *for*. You might simply extend the picture posters already made for *of* by attaching another piece of paper to each and writing the word *for* and the name of one of the children in your class. Underline the *for* and your posters now look like this:

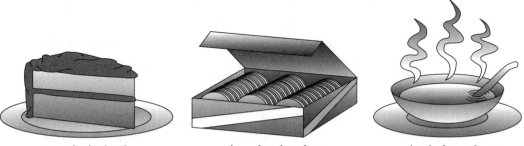

a piece <u>of</u> cake <u>for</u> Thomas   a box <u>of</u> cookies <u>for</u> Tammy   a bowl <u>of</u> soup <u>for</u> Negumi

Have children name foods and tell who they are for; then provide chanting and writing practice with both the words *for* and *of*.

When *of* and *for* are firmly associated and can be read and written, teach *from*. For each difficult word, think of some picture or sentence association your children would understand. Perhaps you have some children who came to your school from other states or countries. You could make some sentence posters with sentences such as:

Billy is *from* California.

José is *from* Mexico.

The children can then associate meaning with the word *from* because they know where these two classmates come from. Then provide practice with *of, for,* and *from.*

How much meaning you have to build for words and how much practice will be required to learn this varies with the different words and for different children. In general, the more abstract a word is and the more similar-looking abstract words there are, the more association and practice will be required to learn them. The three principles for teaching the frequently occurring word are:

1. Provide a way for students to associate meaning with the words.
2. Once meaning is associated, provide practice using a variety of learning modes.
3. If a common word has many confusable words, teach one first. As soon as that one is learned, teach another and practice both. Then, teach a third and practice all three.

Doing a Word Wall

Children need to associate meaning with the abstract connecting words, and they need to have them displayed in some readily accessible place so that they can find them when they need them while reading and writing. Many teachers display these words on the wall or on a bulletin board. They "have" a word wall. For struggling readers, having a word wall is not sufficient. You have to "do" the word wall.

Doing the Word Wall is not the same thing as having a word wall. Having a word wall might mean putting all these words up somewhere in the room and telling students to use them. Most struggling readers can't use them because they don't know them and don't know which is which! Doing a Word Wall means:

1. being selective and limiting the words to those really common words that children need a lot in writing
2. adding words gradually—five a week

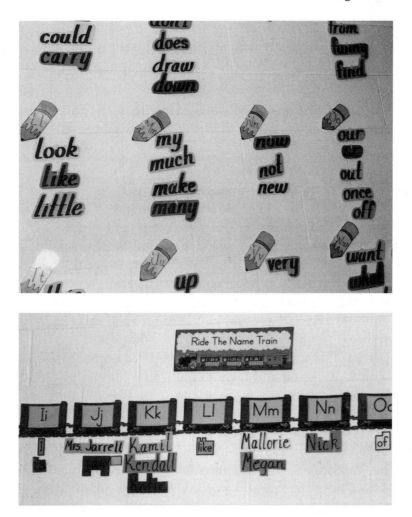

Here are two word walls from primary classrooms. Teachers often begin their word wall by gradually adding the names of the children in the class and then beginning to add the high-frequency words.

3. making words accessible by putting them where everyone can see them, writing them in big black letters, and using a variety of colors so that the constantly confused words (*for, from; that, them, they, this,* etc.) have different colors

4. practicing the words by chanting and writing them, because struggling readers are not usually good visual learners and can't just look at and remember words

5. doing a variety of review activities to provide enough practice so that the words are read and spelled instantly and automatically
6. making sure that Word-Wall Words are spelled correctly in any writing students do

Teachers who "do" word walls (rather than just have word walls) report that ALL their children can learn these critical words.

Selecting Words for the Wall

The selection of the words varies from classroom to classroom, but the selection principle is the same. We include words students will need often in their reading and writing and that are often confused with other words. First-grade teachers who are using a reading series usually select some highly frequent words taught in those books. Other teachers select their words from a high-frequency word list. In addition to high-frequency words, first-grade teachers often begin their word walls with the names of their children and add an example word for each letter in the alphabet—even if there is no high-frequency word for that letter.

Beyond first grade, we look for words commonly misspelled in the children's writing and add them to the wall. Children frequently misspell homophones, and these can be added with a picture or phrase clue attached to all but one of the words. For example, we add a card with the number 2 next to *two* and attach the word *also* and the phrase *too late* next to *too*. Children learn to think about whether they are writing the number *two*, the "too late *too*," or "the other one." Once high-frequency words are on the wall, teachers may add words with a particular pattern—beginning letters, rhyming pattern, vowel pattern, ending—to provide an example for this pattern.

Displaying the Words

The words are written with a thick, black-ink, permanent marker on pieces of different colored paper. Words are placed on the wall above or below the letter they begin with. When confusable words are added, we make sure they are on a different color paper from the other words they are usually confused with. Cutting around the configuration is another helpful cue to those confusable words. Children who are looking for *where* tend to distinguish it from *were* by its "*h* sticking up." Most teachers add five new words each week and do at least one daily activity in which the children find, chant, and write the words.

Chanting and Writing the Words

To begin the word wall practice, students number a sheet of paper from one to five. The teacher calls out five words, putting each word in a sentence. As the teacher calls out each word, a child finds and points to that word on the wall. Next, the students clap and chant the spelling of each word in a rhythmic fashion. After chanting, they write each word. Many teachers tie this daily writing of five words into handwriting instruction and model for the children how to make each letter as the children write the words. When all five words have been written, the teacher leads the students to check or fix their own papers. On the day new words are

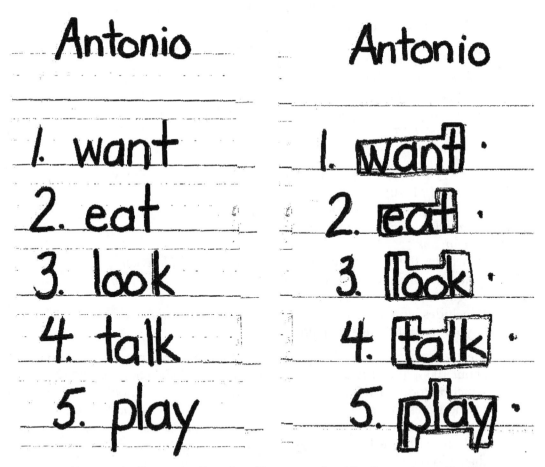

Here are the five word-wall words written on one day. After the words are all written, the words are checked. In this classroom, they trace around each word to make sure the letters are correctly made.

High-Utility Wall Words

Teachers make their own decisions about which words to add to their word walls by observing which words children use frequently in their writing. This list is intended to be an example of the kinds of words that might be included if the word wall is to have the highest utility for the children. This list has high utility in multiple ways:

It includes the most frequent words—those that make up 50 percent of the words children read and write.

There is an example word for each initial consonant: *b, c, d, f, g, h, j, k, l, m, n, p, r, s, t, v, w, y, z* (including both common sounds for *c* and *g*).

There is an example for the most common blends: *bl, br, cl, cr, dr, fl, fr, gr, pl, pr, sk, sl, sm, sn, sp, st, str*, and *tr*; the common digraphs *ch, sh, th, wh*; and the two-letter combinations *ph, wr, kn, qu*.

There is an example for the most common vowel spelling patterns:

> *at, make, rain, day, car, saw, caught*
> *went, eat, see, her, new*
> *in, like, night, girl, thing*
> *not, those, coat, go, for, how, slow, out, boy, look, school*
> *us, use, hurt*
> *my, very*

There is an example for the highest-utility phonograms (Wylie & Durrell, 1970):

> *ack; ail; ain; ake; ale; ame; an; ank; ap; ash; at; ate; aw; ay; eat; ell; est; ice; ick; ide; ight; ill; in; ine; ing; ink; ip; it; ock; oke; op; ore; ot; uck; ug; ump; unk.*

It includes the most common contractions: *can't, didn't, don't, it's, won't*, and the most common homophones: *to, too, two; their, they're, there; right, write; no, know; one, won*.

It includes words such as *favorite, teacher, school, family*, and *sister*, which young children use frequently in their writing.

Ideally, a classroom word wall would add five words per week and have about 100–120 words by the end of the year. This list contains 180 words, which is too many for any one word wall. In some schools, first-grade teachers pick the most frequent words for their walls. Second-grade teachers begin the year by gradually putting up some of the first-grade words that are particularly hard to spell—*they, were, because*, and so forth—and then add others.

about	don't	it	phone	they're
after	down	it's	play	thing
all	drink	joke	presents	this
am	each	jump	pretty	those
an	eat	junk	question	time
and	family	kick	rain	to
animal	father	know	ride	too
are	favorite	like	right	trip
as	first	line	run	truck
at	fly	little	said	two
be	for	long	sale	up
because	friend	look	saw	us
been	from	made	school	use
best	fun	mail	see	very
big	get	make	she	want
black	girl	many	sister	was
boy	give	me	slow	way
brother	go	more	skate	we
bug	good	mother	small	went
but	green	my	snap	were
by	gym	name	so	what
call	had	new	some	when
can	has	nice	sports	where
can't	have	night	stop	which
car	he	no	street	who
caught	her	not	talk	why
children	here	now	teacher	will
city	him	of	tell	with
clock	his	off	than	won
coat	house	old	thank	won't
come	how	on	that	would
could	hurt	one	the	write
crash	I	or	their	you
day	if	other	them	your
did	in	out	then	zoo
didn't	into	over	there	
do	is	people	they	

added, the new words are called out, clapped, chanted, and written. These new words are often reviewed on the second day. During the rest of the week, however, any five words from the wall can be called out. Words with which children need much practice are called out almost every day.

"On the Back" Activities

Most teachers allot 10 minutes each day for the daily word wall practice. Early in the year, it takes the whole 10 minutes to call out, chant, write, and check five words. As the year goes on, children become much faster at chanting, writing, and checking the words and can do five words in 5–6 minutes. At this point, we add an "on the back" activity (called this because we have them turn over their word-wall paper and do this activity on the back). The on-the-back activity is designed to provide additional practice with word-wall words or to help children learn that some of the words on the wall can help them spell lots of other words. Several of the most popular and productive on-the-back activities are described below.

Easy Rhyming Activity

Half the high-frequency words do not follow the logical patterns—but half do. Many teachers put a star or sticker on word-wall words that children can use to help them spell lots of rhyming words. This activity helps children learn how to use the starred words to spell lots of other words. To begin this activity, the teacher might say something like:

> "All of the words we have on our word wall are important words because we see them over and over again in the books we read and they help us write. But some words are important in another way. Some of the words on our wall will help us spell lots of other words that rhyme with them. *It* is one of those helpful words."

The teacher circles *it,* which was one of the five words called out today.

> "Today, we are going to practice using *it* to spell five other words we use a lot in our writing. Turn your paper over and number from one to five. The first word *it* will help you spell is *bit*. You might be writing about how your brother got **bit** by a dog. Let's say *bit* slowly and listen for the first sound. Yes, *bit* begins with the letter *b*. Everyone write *b*. Now, words that rhyme usually have the same spelling pattern. The spelling pattern in a short word begins with the vowel and continues until the end of the word. Because *it* begins with a vowel, *i*, the whole word *it* is also the spelling pattern. Write *i-t* after *b* and you can spell *bit*."

The on-the-back lesson continues as the teacher gives them possible scenarios in which they would need to use *it* to help them spell a rhyming word:

> "What if you were writing about the baseball game and wanted to say you got a **hit**. Say *hit* slowly. Write the first letter, *h,* and then finish the rhyming word with the spelling pattern *i-t*."

> "You might be writing about how you taught your dog to **sit**." Everyone writes s-i-t.

> "You might write about going to the mall to buy a new winter jacket because last year's jacket wouldn't **fit**."

> "The last rhyming word is one that begins with two letters. What if you're writing about your cat and want to tell that when she is really mad, she will **spit** at something. Say *spit* slowly with me, stretching it out and listening for two sounds at the beginning. Good, you hear an *s* and a *p*. Now finish your word with the *i-t* pattern."

For the on-the-back rhyming activity, we have children write five words which we choose that rhyme with one of the word-wall words. We put it in a "What if you are writing and need to spell" context because knowing how rhyming words help you spell other words is only useful if you do it when you are writing and trying to spell a word. We use several examples, trying to choose words they might actually need to write. In most lessons, we include some words with single beginning letters and others where you have to listen for two letters. We model how you "stretch out the word," listening for the beginning sound, and then finish the word with the spelling pattern—the vowel and what follows.

If you have the word *eat* on your word wall, you might have students spell rhyming words by having them pretend they are writing sentences such as:

> I hope Wake will **beat** Carolina this Saturday.
> We had a storm, and the **heat** was off at my house.
> We had company, and I had to get my room clean and **neat**.
> I was good at school, so my Dad took me to the mall for a **treat**.
> Some kids will try to **cheat** to win the game.

When you do these rhyming activities, be sure to give them the rhyming word rather than ask them to tell you rhyming words. Some rhymes have more than one pattern, and by controlling which words you have them spell, you can avoid using words such as *feet* and *Pete*, which have another pattern. They will eventually have to learn to use their visual checking

Here are the rhyming words with *play* written on the back of the word-wall paper.

system to determine the correct pattern, but the first step is to get them spelling by pattern rather than putting down one letter for each sound. Here are a few more examples for starred words from the word wall.

At will help you spell *cat, bat, hat, brat,* and *flat.*
Look will help you spell *cook, book, hook, brook,* and *crook.*
Went will help you spell *bent, dent, tent, sent,* and *spent.*
Not will help you spell *hot, got, lot, spot,* and *trot.*
Am will help you spell *ham, Sam, Pam, clam,* and *Spam.*
And will help you spell *hand, sand, band, stand,* and *brand.*

Can will help you spell *Dan, man, ran, tan,* and *plan.*
Will will help you spell *Bill, fill, pill, still,* and *spill.*
Make will help you spell *bake, cake, rake, lake,* and *shake.*

Harder Rhyming Activity

There is another rhyming "on-the-back" format that is harder but closer to what children actually have to do to use the word-wall words to spell a word they need while writing. To do this rhyming format, make sure that all the words you call out for them to write on the front have some words that rhyme and share the same spelling pattern. You might call out the words *make, thing, like, went,* and *will.* Help the children to notice that all these words are helpful words (starred or stickered words if they are so on your wall). Tell them that you are going to pretend to be writing and need to spell a word that rhymes with one of these five words. Tell them some sentences you might be writing, emphasizing the word you need to spell, and let them decide which of the five helpful words they wrote on the front will help you.

We like to cook chicken on the **grill.**
I was so scared I started to **shake** all over.
My brother **spent** his whole allowance on baseball cards.
We are going to **sing** at my church on Sunday morning.
I want a new **bike** for my birthday.

Once you have begun to use this new rhyming format, alternate it with the easier one in which your sentences use rhymes for only one of the words. The harder one helps children who are ready to learn how thinking of a rhyming word can help them spell lots of words. The easier format is still important for children who are still developing their sense of rhyme and how rhyme helps us spell.

Easy Ending Activity

Another on-the-back activity helps children learn how to spell word-wall words that need an ending. Imagine that the five word-wall words you called out for them to locate, cheer for, and write were:

girl
boy
friend
brother
sister

Have them turn their papers over and write the words *boys, sisters, brothers, friends,* and *girls.*

On another day, call out five words that can have *ed* endings, such as *want, look, jump, kick,* and *play.* Then, have them write these words with the *ed* ending on the back. On another day, do a similar activity with words to which *ing* can be added.

For the easy endings activities, we limit the ending to just one, and we don't include words that need spelling changes. Once students get good at adding *s, ed,* and *ing,* we do some more complex on-the-back activities with endings.

Harder Ending Activity

Make your on-the-back activity with endings more complex by including different words and endings. Imagine that your students have written these five words on the front of their paper:

want

eat

look

talk

play

Have them turn their papers over. Then say something like:

> Today we are going to work on how to spell these word-wall words when they need a different ending. I will say some sentences that some of you might write, and you listen for the word-wall word that has had an ending added:

My friends and I love **eating** at McDonald's.

We were **looking** for some new shoes.

I was **talking** on the phone to my Grandma.

My mom **wants** the new baby to be a girl.

My friend spent the night and we **played** Nintendo till 11:00.

After each sentence, the children identify the word-wall word and the ending, decide how to spell it, and write it on their papers.

As the children get good at adding *s, ed,* and *ing,* include some endings with spelling changes—the *e* dropped, a *y* changed to *i,* or a letter doubled. Since the teacher and children decide ahead of time what to write, everyone is writing them correctly, and this additional information about how to spell words with a variety of endings and spelling changes really moves the accelerated learners along in their writing ability.

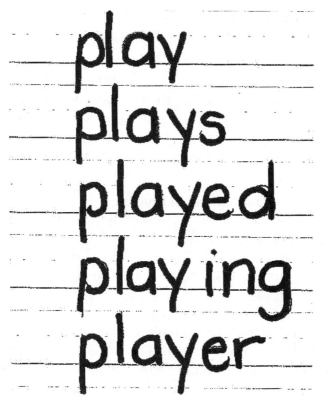

An on-the-back activity with endings added to *play*.

When students are good at spelling word-wall words with the most common endings, include some words in which *y*, *ly*, *er*, and *est* are added. Show them how they can spell *jumpy*, *rainy*, and *funny* by adding *y* to *jump*, *rain*, and *fun*, and how to spell *nicely* and *friendly* by adding *ly*. You can add *er* and *est* to *new*, *little*, and *pretty*. *Talk*, *jump*, *kick*, *ride*, *make*, *eat*, and *quit* can become the person who does them by adding *er*. Of course, you will help them decide what spelling changes they need as they write these words.

Combining Rhyme and Endings

Once your children are good at spelling words that rhyme with word-wall words and adding endings, it is time to combine these two formats. Begin with an easy rhyming format in which the words rhyme with just one word-wall word and have endings added. Here is an example using the word-wall word, *down*. The sentences the teacher says in which the children need to identify a word with an ending that rhymes with *down* might be:

My favorite thing at the circus was the **clowns**.
I saw the teacher **frowning** at me.

In the play, I was **crowned** the king.
My little brother fell in the pool and almost **drowned**.
I have lived in three different **towns**.

You could also do this with the harder format. When children are writing, they often need to spell a word that rhymes with one of the word-wall words and has an ending added. Make sure, however, that everyone spells the word aloud correctly before writing it, because this could be frustrating for many of your children. The children have written the words *tell*, *school*, *but*, *make*, and *rain* on the front.

My sister won the third-grade **spelling** bee.
We almost had a wreck when the **brakes** didn't work on our truck.
I **trained** my dog to stay when I tell him to.
My brother makes money **cutting** all the lawns in the neighborhood.
I am going swimming as soon as the **pools** open.

Be a Mind Reader

Be a Mind Reader is a favorite on-the-back activity. In this game, the teacher thinks of a word on the wall and then gives five clues to that word. Choose a word and write it on a scrap of paper, but do not let the students see what word you have written. Have students number their paper one to five, and tell them that you are going to see who can read your mind and figure out which of the words on the board you are thinking of and have written on your paper. Tell them you will give them five clues. By the fifth clue, everyone should guess your word, but if they read your mind they might get it before the fifth clue. For your first clue, always give the same clue: "It's one of the words on the wall." Students should write next to number one the word they think it might be. Each succeeding clue should narrow down what it can be until by clue five there is only one possible word. As you give clues, students write the word they believe it is next to each number. If succeeding clues confirm the word a student has written next to one number, the student writes that word again by the next number. Clues may include any features of the word you want students to notice. (It has more than two letters. It has less than four letters. It has an *e*. It does not have a *t*.) After clue five, show students the word you wrote on your scratch paper and say, "I know you all have the word next to number five, but who has it next to number four? Three? Two? One?" Some students will have read your mind and will be pleased as punch with themselves!

1. It's one of the words on the wall.
2. It has four letters.

3. It begins with *th.*
4. The vowel is an *e.*
5. It finishes the sentence *I gave my books to __.*

Ruler Tap

A ruler is used for another activity. The teacher calls out a word and then taps out several letters in that word without saying those letters. When the tapping stops, the teacher calls on a child to finish spelling the word out loud. If the child correctly finishes spelling the word, that child gets to call out a word and tap some of the letters. Everyone writes each word after each word is tapped and spelled.

OTHER WORD WALL PRACTICE ACTIVITIES

In addition to the on-the-back activities that take just a few minutes of time after students write five words on the front, there are two popular activities that take a little longer but help students practice these critical high-frequency words. The children see both WORDO and the Word Sorts as games and often ask to play them during indoor recess.

WORDO

WORDO is a variation of the ever-popular Bingo game. Children love it and don't know they are getting a lot of practice reading and writing highly frequent words. All you need to play WORDO is some photocopied sheets on which 9 or 25 blocks have been drawn in, and some small pieces of paper, or objects, for students to use to cover words as they fill in the blocks. Reproduce a good supply of these grid sheets and you are ready when the assembly program is canceled or the foreign language teacher suddenly quits.

Call on students to pick words from the wall they want included in the game. As each word is picked, students will write it on their WORDO sheets in a blank block they choose, and you will write it on an index card. (Make sure students understand that unlike its Bingo counterpart, all children will ultimately have all the same words that are called out. Since they will have written them in different places, however, there will still be winners. Unfortunately, you can't play for a full card.)

When all students have filled up their sheets with the 9 or 25 words called out, you are ready to play. Shuffle your index cards and call the words one at a time. Have students chant the spelling of each word and then cover it with paper squares or small objects. The first student to have

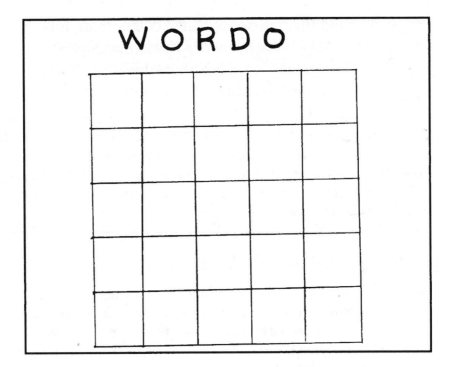

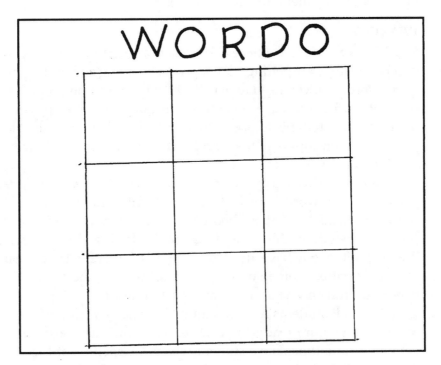

WORDO

a complete row covered wins WORDO. Be sure to have the winner tell you the words covered and check to see that the words have been called. Students can then clear their sheets and play again. You might let the winner become the next caller and you can play the winner's sheet. Children love watching their teachers lose.

Word Sorts

Word sorts can be done with the words on the wall or any group of words the teacher wants students to concentrate on. The purpose of word sorts is to focus student attention on the various features of the words. To do a word sort, write 10–15 words on large index cards and have students write these words on separate slips of paper. Have the students sort the words into different piles, depending on some features certain words share. Students may sort all words with a certain number of letters, all words that begin with a certain letter, or all words that have a certain letter anywhere in them.

Sometimes, the teacher tells the students the criterion on which to sort, for example, all words with an *a* in them. Other times, the teacher tells students which words to select—*boy, try, my, day*—and the students must guess how these words are all alike. In this case, these are all words that end in the letter *y*. Sorting words based on the number of letters and on the different letters and sounds represented by the letters helps students attend to those letters.

Words can also be sorted according to semantic features. Students might choose all the things or all the words that name people. Words that describe things, words that tell what you can do, words that name things found outside are just some of the many possibilities for sorting based on semantic features. Once students understand the various ways the words can be sorted, they can play the role of teacher and tell which words to choose or a criterion for sorting the words.

PORTABLE WORD WALLS

Portable word walls were invented by an enterprising remedial-reading teacher whose third graders complained that they couldn't "write good" in her room because they didn't have their word wall. Upon investigation, it was discovered that their classroom teacher had a colorful word wall and that these remedial readers used the wall to spell highly frequent words as they wrote. Any thought of constructing a word wall in the remedial teacher's room was quickly dismissed when the teacher remembered her room was really a closet and that other teachers used this space. The problem was solved by constructing portable word walls made of file folders divided alphabetically. The classroom teacher, the remedial teacher, and the students worked together to copy all the words on the wall to the folders, using permanent markers the same color as the paper on which wall words were written. Then, each week, as five words were added to the classroom word wall, the teacher and students added them to their portable word walls. The students took their word walls to remedial reading and home for the summer. Perhaps, they even took them to fourth grade the next year.

Portable word walls are also used by some teachers in addition to the word walls in the classroom. Some teachers reproduce a sheet and send it home each week or month with the new words added. Students are told to have their portable word wall out as they do homework because "word-wall" words must be spelled correctly in everything you write.

PortableWW

A	B	C	D	E	F
are	before	can't	don't	enough	first
also		could			favorite
about					

G	H	I	J	K	L
getting	have	I'm		know	let's
		into		knew	

M	N	O	P	Q	R
myself	new	one	people		really
		our			

S	T	U	V	W	X	YZ
said	then	until	very	want		your
school	there			was		you're
	threw			wear		
	to			whether		

A portable word wall made from a file folder.

Portable Word Wall—August/September

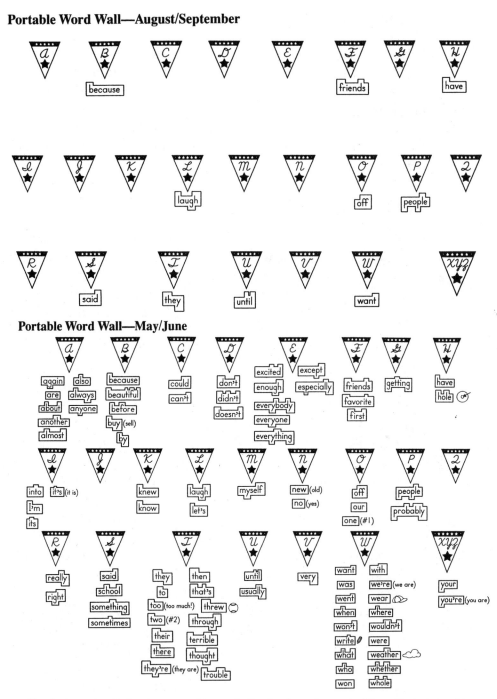

Portable Word Wall—May/June

The first word-wall sheet was sent home in September when only 10 particularly troublesome words had been added to this fourth-grade classroom's word wall. Words were gradually added until the end of the year when the final word wall sheet went home.

From *Month-by-Month Phonics for Upper Grades.* (Cunningham & Hall, 1998) Material appears courtesy of Carson-Dellosa Publishing Company, Inc.

THEME BOARDS

Word wall space is reserved for really important words—words we want all students to learn to read and spell automatically, fluently, correctly, every time, everywhere! In every classroom there are other words students need—but the need changes as units, topics, and themes change. In addition to a word wall, most elementary classrooms have a theme board on which to display these words. The words on the board change as units, topics, and themes change.

HOW A WORD WALL IS MULTILEVEL

If you watched children doing the daily word-wall practice, you might assume that they are all learning the same thing—how to spell words. But what they are doing externally may not reveal what they are processing internally. Imagine that the five new words added to the wall one week were *come, where, they, boy, friend.* During the daily word-wall practice, the children who have already learned to read them are learning to spell them. Other children, however, who require lots of practice with words, are learning to read them. Once each child has practiced them enough to be able to read them (the length of time varies from child to child and word to word), the same daily word-wall practice will help them learn to spell the words.

On-the-back activities that extend word-wall words to the spelling of rhyming words and words with endings provide something to be learned for your accelerated students. Teachers who do these activities regularly report that the best readers in the class not only spell all the word-wall words correctly but spell uncommon rhyming words and words with endings. If you practice handwriting each day as you write the word-wall words, all children get some handwriting instruction—often needed by both struggling and advanced readers.

Once you have a word wall growing in your room, it will be evident that your students use it as they are reading and writing. You will see their eyes quickly glance to the exact spot where a word they want to write is displayed. You will hear them say: "I need that *too;* that is the 'me too' *too.*" Or "*Where* starts with *w* and is the red word with the *h* sticking up." Even when children are reading, they will sometimes glance over to the word wall to help them remember a particularly troublesome word.

Word walls provide children with an immediately accessible dictionary for the most troublesome words. Because the words are added

Here are two theme boards from primary classrooms.

March Words

wind	sunny	Easter
storm	good luck	vacation
kite	flowers	rabbit
tornado	daffodils	bunny
severe weather	crocus	hop hun
lion	Japan	rainbow
lamb	leprechaun	beach
St. Patrick's Day	bloom	short sleeve
clovers	green grass	dying eggs
Spring	Dr. Seuss	chocolate
birthdays	green eggs	basket
bird	ham	candy
blows	gold	colors
butterflies	pot	sunflower seeds

gradually, stay in the same spot forever, are listed alphabetically by first letter, are made visually distinctive by different colors of paper and by cutting around the configuration, and because of the daily practice in finding, chanting , and writing these words, almost all children learn to read and spell almost all the words. Because the words you selected are words they need constantly in their reading and writing, their recognition of these words becomes automatic, and their limited attention can be devoted to the less frequent words and to constructing meaning as they read and write.

FLUENCY COMES FROM LOTS OF EASY READING AND DAILY WRITING

Making sure your children associate meaning with the abstract connecting words and doing a word wall are important steps in helping all children learn to read and spell these words. But, if you want all your children to be fluent readers and writers, you must also provide for lots of easy reading and daily writing.

Fluency is fast, expressive reading. The easiest way to imagine fluency is to remember what a nonfluent reader sounds like. Some children read one word at a time, hes si ta ting and re peat ing words. In the previous sentence, I have tried to remind you what a nonfluent reader sounds like. Every teacher has had the experience of working with children who can read most words but for whom reading is a tortured, labored, word-by-word, sometimes syllable-by-syllable process. Children who lack fluency generally only read when they have to and have not developed the automatic and immediate identification of words that lots of reading leads to. There is an almost certain prescription for developing fluency—lots of very easy reading and daily writing!

Imagine that in this new millennium, when all kinds of technological wonders are being invented and mass-marketed, someone invents a readowritometer. This marvelous device, when implanted in a child's brain, would tally up the number of words that child read or wrote across all the home and school hours—school days and weekends. Imagine that various children had their readowritometers constantly running for their first three years of school. At the end of these three years, the children would all be given a test that would determine how many words they could immediately recognize and how fast and accurate they were at figuring out how to pronounce and spell unfamiliar words. The number of words read and written would be an incredibly good predictor of each child's word fluency. Children who read and wrote a lot would instantly recognize huge numbers of words and be much faster and more accurate at decoding and spelling than children who read little. The first and most important component of good word instruction is large doses of successful reading and writing. Here is how successful teachers make sure this happens.

Schedule Daily Self-Selected Reading

Self-Selected Reading is a critical daily component of a balanced reading program in any classroom. Some significant amount of time every day in every classroom should be devoted to children choosing for themselves something to read and then settling down to read it. Self-selected reading is often promoted in terms of the motivation and interest children develop as they have time to pursue their own personal interests through books. In addition, the amount of reading children do is the biggest variable in their word fluency, and children who engage in regular self-selected reading read a lot more than children who don't.

All a teacher of young children has to do to have a successful self-selected reading program is to provide a good reading model through daily teacher read-aloud, schedule time each day for children to read in books they choose, and provide lots of different books on all different levels and of all different types. For older children—particularly children who are not fluent readers—it is not so easy. These nonfluent older readers don't think of themselves as good readers and don't want to read the easy books they deem "baby books."

Linda Fielding and Cathy Roller attack this "baby book attitude" head on in a 1992 *Reading Teacher* article, "Making Difficult Books Accessible and Easy Books Acceptable." Among the ideas for making difficult books accessible are:

1. Provide independent reading time when children can self-select books (including nonfiction) and interact with others about what they learn from these books.
2. Read difficult books to the children.
3. Partner the children, putting a more able reader with a less able reader.
4. Provide lots of rereading opportunities because difficult material becomes easier each time it is read.
5. Precede difficult books on a topic with easier books on that topic to build background knowledge.

All these suggestions will help children read with more fluency even when the material they are reading is more difficult than it should optimally be.

Among their many practical ideas for making easy books acceptable Fielding and Roller suggest:

1. Modeling, by reading aloud, the use and enjoyment of easy books.
2. Altering purposes for easy reading by having older children read these books to younger buddies.
3. Allowing children to make tape recordings of favorite books.
4. Making the expanding world of nonfiction books readily available.

I have seen all four of these strategies successfully used and even a combination that worked like this: A fourth-grade teacher with many children still reading—not very fluently—at first- and second-grade levels decided that the children needed to do lots of easy reading. She partnered each child with a kindergartner and arranged for a weekly reading time. She then gathered up a lot of easy books, including many Dr. Seuss titles, Clifford books, and many nonfiction picture books (including alphabet books, some of which are listed in Chapter 1). Across the course of a week or two, she read these books to her children and let each child choose one book to prepare to read to the kindergarten buddy. When the children had chosen their books, they practiced reading the book several times—with a partner—to the tape recorder—and finally to the teacher. By the time her children trotted down to the kindergarten—easy books proudly in hand—all the children were fluent readers of their book.

On their return to the fourth-grade classroom, they talked about their experience with their kindergarten buddies and whether or not their book was a good choice. The teacher made a chart on which each child listed the book read aloud that week. The following day, the teacher and the children gathered and reviewed the chart showing who had read what. The teacher also reminded them of some other books no one had chosen the first week and led them to choose their second book. The partner reading, tape-recorder reading, and reading to the teacher continued as it had for the first week except that, if a child chose a book which another child had read the previous week, that child became the "expert" on that book and read the book to or listened to the new reader read the book at least once. The second trip to the kindergarten went more smoothly than the first, and the children returned, discussed the kindergartners' responses to the books, and listed the second book they had read on the chart.

By the fourth week, the easy-reading-for-fluency program was up and running with minimal help from the teacher. Many children chose books their friend had chosen previously, and they enjoyed reading together and often tape recording the book together in preparation for performing their weekly "civic volunteer" duty.

Easy reading is essential for children to develop fluency. This easy reading can be accomplished and legitimized in a variety of ways. Another wonderful *Reading Teacher* article I recommend to anyone concerned with fluency is "The 'Curious George' Strategy for Students With Reading Problems" (Richek & McTague, 1988). In this article, the authors describe how they used assisted reading and a series of books—in this case the Curious George books—to help some second- and third-grade remedial readers develop reading fluency, confidence, and enjoyment.

Assisted reading (Hoskisson, 1975) is what it sounds like. The teacher assists a group of children through repeated readings of some text. Usually, the teacher reads the text the first time, the children chime in with known words the second time, and rereading continues as the children take over more and more of the reading. This article brings a new twist to assisted reading by using the popular Curious George series. The teacher assisted the children in reading many books in the series, and as they read more and more books, most children were able to—and preferred to—do the initial reading of one of the later-used Curious George books on their own.

In addition to repeated reading and assisted reading, choral reading is a time-tested strategy that will help children become fluent readers. To do choral reading, most teachers begin with a piece of poetry or a chant the children are familiar with. The material for choral reading should be duplicated or put on a chart or overhead to make the print visible to everyone. Next, decide which parts everyone—the chorus—should read and which parts will make good solos, and assign parts and solos. You will need to practice the piece several times—with the readers becoming more fluent each time. Be sure to emphasize how to speak dramatically, and include some sound effects if the piece allows that. Once you have practiced several times, perform the choral reading for a group or make a video or audio tape of your performance.

All kinds of poems and chants can be used for choral reading. Children respond particularly well to the rhymes in Joanna Cole's *Anna Banana: 101 Jump Rope Rhymes* (1989) and to the book Cole wrote with Stephanie Calmenson, *Miss Mary Mack and Other Children's Street Rhymes* (1990). Another great source for "kid-pleasing" choral readings is Ruth Dowell's *Let's Talk!* (1986).

Coach Children to Use Strategies During Oral Reading

Most of the reading children do should be silent reading where the focus is on understanding and enjoying what they read. It is also helpful and fun for children to have times when they read aloud. Young children like to read aloud, and as they are reading aloud, teachers have a chance to see how they are using their strategies and to coach them. When children read aloud, they always produce a few misreadings. It is these misreadings that allow teachers a "window on the reading process " of the reader. It is in responding to these misreadings that teachers have a chance to coach children into strategic reading. Here are some suggestions for making oral reading an enjoyable and profitable endeavor.

Have Children Read to Themselves Before Reading Orally   Making sure that silent reading for comprehension precedes oral reading will ensure that students do not lose track of the fact that reading is first and foremost to understand and react to the meaning of the printed words. Young children who are just beginning to read should also read material to themselves or with a partner before reading it orally to a group or the teacher. When beginning readers read, however, it is seldom silent. They don't yet know how to think the words in their minds, and their reading to themselves can be described as "mumble" or "whisper" reading.

Use Easy Material for Oral Reading   Material that students read orally should be easy enough that they will make no more than five errors per hundred words read. If the average sentence length is seven words, this would be no more than one error every three sentences. It is very important that children not make too many errors, because their ability to cross-check drops dramatically when they are making so many errors that they can't make sense of it.

Don't Let Children Correct Each Other   Allowing students to interrupt and correct each other inhibits the reader's ability to self-correct and forces the reader to try for "word-perfect reading." While it might seem that striving for word-perfect reading would be a worthy goal, it is not, because of the way our eyes move when we read.

When you read, your eyes move across the line of print in little jumps. The eyes then stop and look at the words. The average reader can see about 12 letters at a time—one large word, two medium words, or three small words. When your eyes stop, they can see only the letters they have stopped on. The following letters are not visible until the eyes move forward and stop once again. Once your eyes have moved forward, you can't see the words you saw during the last stop. As you read orally, your eyes move out ahead of your voice. This is how you can read with expression, because the intonation and emphasis you give to a particular word can be determined only when you have seen the words that follow it. The space between where your eyes are and where your voice is we call your eye-voice span. Fluent readers reading easy material have an eye-voice span of five to six words.

Good readers read with expression because their voice is trailing their eyes. When they say a particular word, their eyes are no longer on that word but rather several words down the line. This explains something that all good readers do. They make little non-meaning-changing errors when they read orally. They read *can't* when the actual printed words were *can not*. They read *car* when the actual printed word was *automobile*. Non-meaning-changing errors are a sign of good reading! They indicate that the eyes are out there ahead of the voice, using the later words in the sentence to confirm the meaning, pronunciation, and expression given to previous words. The reader who says "car" for *automobile* must have correctly recognized or decoded *automobile* or that reader could not have substituted the synonym *car*. When the reader says "car," the word *automobile* can no longer be seen because the eyes have moved on.

Good readers make small non-meaning-changing errors because their eyes are not right on the words they are saying. If other children are allowed to follow along while the oral reader reads, they will interrupt the reader to point out these errors. If children are allowed to correct non-meaning-changing errors, children learn that when reading orally, you should keep your eyes right on the very word you are saying. This fosters word-by-word reading. Too much oral reading with each error corrected by the children or the teacher will result in children not developing the eye-voice span all good fluent readers have. Constant interruptions by the teacher or other children also work against developing appropriate cross-checking strategies and spontaneous self-corrections.

Eliminating interruptions by other children is not easy but can be accomplished by having all the children not reading put their finger in their books and close them. When one child is reading, the others should not be following along with the words. Rather, they should be listening to the reader read and "following along with the meaning." Instead of correcting the reader, teach students to say, "I didn't understand that part. Would you read that again?"

Ignore Errors That Don't Change Meaning   Small, non-meaning-changing errors, such as "can't" for *can not*, are a sign of good eye-voice span and should not be corrected, even by the teacher.

When the Reader Makes a Meaning-Changing Error—Wait   Control the urge to stop and correct the reader immediately. Rather, wait until the reader finishes the sentence or paragraph. What follows the error is often the information the reader needs in order to self-correct. Students who self-correct errors based on subsequent words read should be praised because they are demonstrating their use of cross-checking while reading. Students who are interrupted immediately never learn to self-correct. Instead, they wait for someone else to correct them. Without self-correcting and self-monitoring, children will never become good readers.

If Waiting Doesn't Work, Coach for Strategies Needed   If the reader continues on beyond the end of the sentence or paragraph without correcting a meaning-changing error, the teacher should stop the reader by saying something like:

> "Wait a minute. You read, 'Then the magician stubbled and fell.'
> Does that make sense?"

The teacher has now reinforced a major understanding all readers must use if they are to decode words well. The word must have the right letters and make sense. The letters in *stubbled* are very close to the letters in *stumbled*, but *stubbled* does not make sense. The teacher should pause and see if the reader can find a way to fix it. If so, the teacher should say,

> "Yes, *stumbled* makes sense. Good. Continue reading."

If not, the teacher points out the *m* before the *b*, or suggests a known rhyming word such as *crumbled* or *tumbled*.

Oral reading provides the "teachable moment"—a time for teachers to help students use the sense of what they are reading and the letter-sound relationships they know. When teachers respond to an error by waiting until a meaningful juncture is reached and responding first with a "Did that make sense?" question, children focus more on meaning and begin to correct their own errors. The rest of the group hear how the teacher responds to the error. As they listen, they learn how they should use "sense" and decoding skills as they are actually reading. Feedback that encourages readers to self-correct and monitor their own reading sends a "You can do it" message.

Include Daily Writing

In addition to lots of reading, lots of writing helps children become better decoders and spellers. This is especially true when young children are encouraged to invent-spell the words they need but haven't yet learned to spell. Clarke (1988) compared the decoding ability of end-of-the-year first graders and found that first graders who had been encouraged to invent-spell in first grade were better at decoding words than first graders from classrooms that emphasized correct spelling. One of the biggest concerns teachers express as they teach young children about sound and letter patterns is that the children don't apply what they know to actually figuring out words while reading. To invent-spell a word, however, you have to apply what you know, because using your letter-sound knowledge is the way you get some letters to represent the word.

Of course, in your classroom, you will be doing a word wall. All students will know what words are on the wall and which word is which. When they write, they will spell words as best they can in first draft—unless it is on the word wall. Word-wall words must be spelled correctly in everything, and your students will spell words like *they*, *friend*, *people*, and *because* correctly rather than logically. With older children who have spelled them wrong so many times that the wrong but logical way has become automatic, you will have to write WW next to any word-wall word you see misspelled anywhere. Give them their paper back and have them correct the WW word and return it to you. They won't like this, but they will change their automatic wrong spellings and they will thank you for it later!

Again, establishing a daily writing time is not difficult with young children. They all have things they want to tell, and if teachers model writing during a minilesson, encourage children to write about what they want to write about, and accept whatever writing they can do, young children delight in writing.

Older, struggling nonfluent readers do not delight in writing! In fact, they will tell you they hate to write. This "I hate to write" attitude can be turned around—but it takes patience and determination.

If you teach older nonfluent readers, you must first convince yourself of the value of their writing. As they write and spell the word-wall words correctly, they will become much faster and fluent at writing these words. As they "stretch out" some words to put down what they want to tell, they will be applying what they are learning about letter patterns and decoding. The more and faster they can write, the better they will like it!

Writing promotes word fluency. If you teach older children who hate to write, start doing a word wall and some of the activities described in the next chapter. Then, schedule daily, short—10 minutes max—writing times. Model how to write by letting them watch you writing a few sentences about something you want to tell them, thinking aloud as you write. After they write, let them share if they choose to by reading or telling what they have written. Let them choose what they want to write about. Emphasize that you are interested in what they want to tell, and as long as they spell word-wall words correctly, they should spell the other words as best they can.

Don't worry about publishing or what the final product looks like until your students get over their "I hate to write" attitudes. Then, you can begin to help them improve their writing and learn to write particular things—including those on the mandated writing tests. (For lots more ideas about helping children learn to write fluently, see *Classrooms That Work*, Cunningham & Allington, 1999.)

REFERENCES

Clarke, L. K. (1988). Invented versus traditional spelling in first graders' writings: Effects on learning to spell and read. *Research in the Teaching of English, 22*, 281–309.

Cole, J., & Calmenson, S. (1990). *Miss Mary Mack and other children's street rhymes.* William Morrow.

Cole, J. (1989). *Anna Banana: 101 jump rope rhymes.* William Morrow.

Cunningham, P. M., & Allington, R. L. (1999). *Classrooms that work: They can all read and write* (2d ed.). New York: Longman.

Cunningham, P. M., & Hall, D. P. (1998). *Month by month phonics for upper grades.* Greenboro, NC: Carson-Dellosa.

Dowell, R. (1986). *Let's talk!* Gryphon House.

Fielding, L., & Roller, C. (1992). Making difficult books accessible and easy books acceptable. *The Reading Teacher, 45*, 678–685.

Fry, E., Fountoukidis, D. L., & Polk, J. K. (1985). *The new reading teacher's book of lists.* Englewood Cliffs, NJ: Prentice-Hall.

Hoskisson, K. (1975). The many faces of assisted reading. *Elementary English, 52*, 653–659.

Richek, M. A., & McTague, B. K. (1988). The 'Curious George' strategy for students with reading problems. *The Reading Teacher, 42*, 220–226.

Wylie, R.E. & Durrell, D.D. (1970). Teaching Vowels through Phonograms. *Elementary English, 47*, 787–791.

3
USING PHONICS AND SPELLING PATTERNS

ost of the words we read and write are one- and two-syllable *regular* words, which, because they are consistent with the rules of spelling and pronunciation, we can decode and spell even if we have not seen them before. Developing the ability to independently read and write most regular words is a complex process and takes time and practice with a variety of activities. This chapter describes activities successfully used by teachers to help all children become independent at decoding and spelling regular one- and two-syllable words.

Chapter 1 described activities that develop phonemic awareness and teach some letter names and sounds. If this knowledge is minimal (or nonexistent) in your students, you are not ready for this chapter but should do some of the activities suggested in Chapter 1. The activities in this chapter assume that children have developed some phonemic awareness and know some letter names and consonant sounds. They are now ready to use this knowledge and learn patterns they can use to decode and spell words.

VOWELS IN THE ENGLISH SPELLING SYSTEM

In English, the vowels are variant and unpredictable. The letter *a* commonly represents the sound in *and, made, agree, art, talk,* and *care.* We have given names to some of these sounds. *And* has a short *a; made* has a long *a; agree* is a schwa; the *a* in *art* is *r* controlled. We don't even have names for the sound *a* represents in *talk* and *care.* Further complicating things are the many words in which *a* doesn't do any of these six common things—*eat, coat, legal*—and the fact that even the consistent sounds can be spelled in many different ways. The long *a* sound is commonly spelled by the patterns in *made, maid,* and *may.* The sound *a* has in *talk* is spelled by an *aw* in *saw* and an *au* in *Paul.*

When you stop to think about all the possible sounds and spelling patterns for the vowels, you marvel that anyone becomes an accurate and fast decoder of English words. Yet that is exactly what happens! All good readers could quickly and accurately pronounce the made-up words *gand, hade, afuse, sart, malk, lare, jeat, foat, pregal, maw,* and *naul.* Just don't ask them to explain how they did it!

In schools we have traditionally taught students many rules and jargon: the *e* on the end makes the vowel long; vowels in unaccented syllables have a schwa sound; when a vowel is followed by *r,* it is *r* controlled. We have taught so many rules and jargon because it takes over 200 rules to account for the common spelling patterns in English. Although these rules describe our English alphabetic system, it is doubtful that readers and writers use these rules to decode and spell words. So how do they do it?

Research (Adams, 1990) supports the view that readers decode words by using spelling patterns from the words they know. *Made, fade, blade,* and *shade* all have the same spelling pattern, and the *a* is pronounced the same in all four. When you see the made-up word *hade,* your mind accesses that known spelling pattern and you give the made-up word the same pronunciation you have for other words with that spelling pattern. Spelling patterns are letters that are commonly seen together in a certain position in words. The *al* at the end of *legal, royal,* and the made-up word *pregal* is a spelling pattern. Sometimes a spelling pattern can be a single letter, as the *a* is in *agree, about, adopt,* and the made-up word *afuse.* Using words you know to decode unknown words is called decoding by analogy.

Spelling patterns are quite reliable indicators of pronunciation—with two exceptions. The first exception was explained in Chapter 2. The most frequently used words are often not pronounced or spelled like other words with that spelling pattern. *To* and *do* should rhyme with *go, so,* and *no. What* should rhyme with *at, cat,* and *bat. They* should be spelled like *way* and *stay. Said* should be spelled like *red* and *bed.* It is precisely because the most frequent words have the least predictable pronunciations and spellings that we use the word wall to help all children learn to read and spell them.

The second exception in spelling patterns is that some spelling patterns have two common sounds. The *ow* at the end of words occurs in *show, grow,* and *slow,* but also in *how, now,* and *cow.* The *ood* at the end of *good, hood,* and *stood* is also found at the end of *food, mood,* and *brood.* Children who are constantly cross-checking meaning with the pronunciations they come up with will not be bothered by these differences, as long as the word they are reading is in their listening-meaning vocabulary.

Whereas spelling patterns work wonderfully well for pronouncing unfamiliar words, they don't work as well for spelling! There are often two or more spelling patterns with the same pronunciation. When trying to read the made-up word *nade,* you would simply compare its pronunciation to other words with that spelling pattern—*made, grade, blade.* If, however, I didn't show you *nade,* but rather pronounced it and asked you to spell it, you might compare it to *maid, paid,* and *braid* and spell it n-a-i-d. Most words can be correctly pronounced by comparing them to known spelling patterns. To spell a word correctly, however, you must often choose between two or more possible spelling patterns. Activities in this chapter will first teach children that you look at the whole pattern to decode and spell words. Once children are decoding and spelling based on patterns, we do two activities—Reading Writing Rhymes and What Looks Right—to help them develop their visual checking system and decide which pattern is the correct spelling.

GUESS THE COVERED WORD

Most short words are made up of two patterns, the beginning letters and the vowel and letters that follow it. The beginning letters (which linguists call onsets and educators call consonants, digraphs, and blends or clusters) are all the letters up to the vowel. Children need to learn the sounds for these letters—which are quite consistent and reliable. Unfortunately, although many children "learn" these sounds—they can circle pictures that begin with them and tell you what letter makes a particular sound if you ask them—they don't use them when they read and write. When writing and trying to figure out the spelling of a word such as *smelly,* they might begin it just with an *s* or an *sl* instead of an *sm.* Faced with an unfamiliar word in their reading, they often guess a word that makes sense but does not begin with the right letters or guess a word with only the correct first letter, ignoring the other letters. All of the activities in this chapter stress learning and using all the beginning letters. Guess the Covered Word lessons teach these beginning letter sounds systematically and teach them in the context of reading. Children learn that guessing just based on beginning letters—or just based on making sense—is not a very good strategy. But when you use all the beginning letters and the sense of the sentence and consider the length of the word, you can make very good guesses at new words.

Here are the beginning letters children need to learn to use. We are using the jargon here—consonants, digraphs, etc.—so that you will recognize what is being taught, but we avoid it "like the plague" with children who get so confused by all the terms, they can't focus on what we want them to—learning and using the sounds of the letters. We teach children the sounds for, and to look and listen for, "all the beginning letters—all the letters up to the vowel."

Single consonants: b c d f g h j k l m n p r s t v w y z (including the "s" sound of *c* in *city* and the "j" sound of *g* in *gym*)

Digraphs (two letters, one sound): sh ch wh th

Other two-letter, one-sound combinations: ph wr kn qu

Blends (beginning letters blended together, sometimes called clusters): bl br cl cr dr fl fr gl gr pl pr sc scr sk sl sm sn sp spr st str sw tr

Guess the Covered Word lessons help students learn to cross-check—to simultaneously think about what would make sense and about letters and sounds. To prepare for a Guess the Covered Word activity, we write 5–7 sentences on the board and cover one word in each sentence. We use sticky notes to cover the words and cover them in such a way that, after three or four guesses are made with no letters showing, we can uncover all the letters up to the vowel. For our first lessons, the sentences follow a similar word pattern, we cover the final word, and we include in our covered words only words that begin with a single initial consonant.

> Kevin wants a pet <u>hamster</u>.
> Mike wants a pet <u>python</u>.
> Paola wants a pet <u>goldfish</u>.
> Ryan wants a pet <u>turtle</u>.
> Devon wants a pet <u>pony</u>.
> Jasmine wants a pet <u>kitten</u>.

We begin the activity by reading the first sentence and asking students to guess the covered word. We write three or four guesses next to the sentence. Pointing out to the children that "It sure can be a lot of words when you can't see any letters," we uncover all the letters up to the vowel (which in these first lessons is only one). We erase guesses that don't begin with that letter and have students suggest possible words that make sense and begin with the correct letter and write these responses. When all the guesses that begin correctly and make sense are written, we uncover the whole word and go on to the next sentence.

We use Guess the Covered Word activities to teach and review all the beginning sounds. As the children begin to understand the strategy they need to use, we don't limit the covered word to the final position. Now they read the whole sentence, skipping the covered word and then coming back to it to make guesses. We follow the same procedure of getting three or four guesses with no letters showing and then uncovering all the letters up to the vowel. Here are some sentences we might use when we are focusing on the digraphs *sh, ch, wh* and *th.*

Corinda likes to eat <u>chicken</u>.
Chad ate <u>thirteen</u> waffles.
Sean likes orange <u>sherbet</u>.
Bob likes strawberry <u>shortcake</u>.
Chris bakes pies for <u>thanksgiving</u>.
Carol likes chocolate <u>cake</u>.

We teach and practice all the blends with Guess the Covered Word activities:

We all love it when it <u>snows</u>.
Some people go <u>skiing</u>.
People ride in <u>snowmobiles</u>.
The <u>snowplow</u> is fun to ride on, too!
You can go down a hill fast in a <u>sled</u>.
Walking back up is hard if the snow is <u>slippery</u>.

Guess the Covered Word is a very versatile strategy. We sometimes use Big Books and cover a word or two on each page. We also write paragraphs summarizing what we have learned during a science or social studies unit and cover words in it.

For years, people have marvelled at the faces of four <u>presidents</u> carved into Mount Rushmore in South Dakota. Now, there is another face to see in the <u>Black</u> Hills. Work on the face of Crazy Horse, a famous Lakota Indian chief, began over <u>fifty</u> years ago. The face of Crazy Horse is <u>huge</u>. It is taller than the <u>Washington</u> Monument. Each eye <u>measures</u> eighteen feet across. All four Mount Rushmore faces could fit inside the <u>face</u> of Crazy Horse. The carving is not <u>fin-ished</u>. <u>Sculptors</u> are now busy carving Crazy Horse's horse for him to ride on. More than one <u>million</u> visitors have already paid the $7 visitor fee to visit the Crazy Horse <u>Memorial</u> and Indian Museum.

Ben is a very ⬚popular⬚ guy.

Justin is a ⬚whiz⬚ at math.

Karen is one of our super ⬚spellers⬚.

David is a ⬚champion⬚ racer.

Paula loves to read ⬚chapter⬚ books.

Tyrone is one of our best ⬚st████████⬚

Mrs. C. thinks she has a ████████ class.

Here is an example of a Guess the Covered Word lesson. They have guessed the first five words, are guessing words that make sense and begin with *st* for the sixth sentence, and have one more to go.

Through Guess the Covered Word activities, children learn that just guessing words is not a good decoding strategy, but when you guess something that makes sense in the sentence, has all the right letters up to the vowel (not just the first one), and is the right length, you can figure out many new words.

CHANGING A HEN TO A FOX

Children love to pretend, and in this activity they pretend they can change one animal, a hen, into a fox. They do this by changing one letter at a time. As they change that letter, they listen for where they hear the changing letter and review all the single consonants. To begin this activity, we write the names of five animals on the board—each of which has a different vowel sound:

cat   hen   pig   fox   bug

The teacher and the children say these words together, stretching out each word and talking about the beginning, middle, and ending sounds. Particular attention is given to the middle sound—the vowel sound—in each of these words. Next the teacher asks the children,

"Can you change a hen into a fox?"

She tells the children that if they follow her directions and think about letters and sounds, they will be able do this. The children all take a sheet of paper and these directions are given.

"Write **hen**" (The teacher points to the word *hen* on the board and everyone copies it onto their papers.)

"Now change the hen to a **pen**." (The teacher and children decide they have to change just the first letter from an *h* to a *p* and write *pen* under *hen*.)

"Now change your pen into a **pet**."(Children decide they have to change the last letter from an *n* to a *t* and write *pet*.).

"Can you change pet to **pit**?" (Teacher helps them stretch out *pit* and decide it is the vowel they need to change and this vowel has the same sound as *pig*.)

"Now change pit to **sit**."

"Next, change sit to **six**."

"Then, change six to **fix**."

"Last, change fix to **fox**."

Children love changing the letters and the animals, and they are using what they are learning about letters and sounds to spell lots of other words. (Many teachers initiate this activity by reading Mem Fox's *Hattie and the Fox* to the children.)

Here are seven other Changing a Hen to a Fox lessons.

pig	bug	pig	cat	fox	bug	cat
rig	dug	big	bat	box	hug	hat
rid	dig	wig	hat	bop	dug	rat
rib	pig	win	rat	top	dig	rag
rob	pin	fin	pat	mop	big	bag
Bob	pen	fit	pet	map	bag	big
box	ten	fat	pen	mat	bat	dig
fox	hen	cat	hen	cat	cat	pig

LEARNING THE MOST COMMON RHYMING PATTERNS

As children are learning the beginning sounds and how they can use these sounds to figure out words, they should also be learning some of the most common rhyming patterns. These rhyming patters are called *rimes* by linguists and often called *word families* or *phonograms* by teachers. We call them *spelling patterns* because we want children to learn that you spell based on patterns—which includes the vowel and the letters that follow. Thirty-seven spelling patterns allow children to read and spell over 500 words commonly used by young children (Wylie & Durrell,1970). Many teachers display these with a word and picture to help children learn the patterns that help them spell many other words.

Here are the 37 high-frequency spelling patterns (with possible key words):

ack (black)	ail (pail)	ain (train)	ake (cake)	ale (whale)
ame (game)	an (pan)	ank (bank)	ap (cap)	ash (trash)
at (cat)	ate (skate)	aw (claw)	ay (tray)	eat (meat)
ell (shell)	est (nest)	ice (rice)	de (bride)	ick (brick)
iight (night)	ill (hill)	in (pin)	ine (nine)	ing (king)
ink (pink)	ip (ship)	it (hit)	ock (sock)	oke (Coke)
op (mop)	ore (store)	ot (hot)	uck (truck)	ug (bug)
ump (jump)	unk (skunk)			

In addition, there are numerous books teachers can read to children and then children can read on their own which contain lots of examples of rhyming words with these most common rhyming patterns. Books with just one rhyming pattern in which almost all the words have the same spelling pattern are the most helpful for children just learning patterns and how they help you spell words. C. and J. Hawkins have written four of these books: *Tog the Dog* (1986), *Jen the Hen* (1985), *Mig the Pig* (1984), and *Pat the Cat* (1993). Rigby publishes a set of Kinderrhymes with 24 titles, including *Rimes with Cat*, *Rimes with Cap* and *Rhymes with King*. *Zoo Looking* by Mem Fox (1995) has lots of words that rhyme with *back*.

Other particularly helpful books are books that contain just 6–8 different rhyming pairs. *There's a Bug in my Mug* and *My Nose Is a Hose*, both by Kent Salisbury (1997), are two such books. Both books contain tabs which when pulled reveal what is in the mug or turn the nose into a hose. These books are great fun and wonderful for helping children begin to understand how rhyming patterns work.

ROUNDING UP THE RHYMES

Rounding Up the Rhymes is an activity to follow up the reading of a book, story, or poem that contains lots of rhyming words. Here is an example using that timeless book, *I Wish That I Had Duck Feet* (Seuss, 1972). The first reading of anything should be for meaning and enjoyment. In Dr. Seuss's *I Wish That I Had Duck Feet*, a boy wishes he had duck feet so that he could splash and wouldn't have to wear shoes until he realizes his mother wouldn't want him in the house like that. The boy goes on to wish for deer horns, a whale spout, a long tail, a long nose until he thinks of the complications each would cause and finally decides to "be just me." As with so many other Seuss books, this one has enormous appeal for children.

After enjoying the book, point out to the children that in addition to a silly story and great illustrations, Dr. Seuss books are fun to read because of all the rhyming words. Tell the children that you are going to read several pages of *I Wish That I Had Duck Feet* again and they can help you "round up the rhymes." Read the first page and have students help you decide that the rhyming words are *why* and *dry*. Write these words on two index cards and place them one under the other in a pocket chart. Read the next page and have the children identify the rhyming words, *me* and *see*. Continue to read until you have six or seven sets of rhyming words.

why	me	brown	play	floor	don't	instead
dry	see	town	way	door	won't	head

Now, reread these pages again. As you get to the rhyming words, point to them in the pocket chart and have the children say them.

Next, have the children help you identify the spelling pattern. Explain that the spelling pattern in a short word includes all the letters beginning with the first vowel and going to the end of the word. After naming the vowels—*a, e, i, o, u,* and sometimes *y*—pick up the first set of rhyming words *why* and *dry*, have the children tell you the spelling pattern in each, and underline the spelling pattern. In *why* and *dry*, the spelling pattern is only the *y*. Put *why* and *dry* back in the pocket chart and pick up the next set of rhymes—*me* and *see*. Have the children say them and hear once more that they do rhyme. Then underline the spelling patterns: *e* and *ee*. They do rhyme but they have a different spelling pattern. Explain that we only want to keep rhymes with the same spelling pattern, then toss *me* and *see* in the trash can.

Continue with the remaining pairs, deciding first that they rhyme and then underlining the spelling pattern to see if it is the same. There are now six pairs of rhyming words with the same spelling pattern in the pocket chart:

wh<u>y</u>	br<u>own</u>	pl<u>ay</u>	fl<u>oor</u>	d<u>on't</u>	inst<u>ead</u>
dr<u>y</u>	t<u>own</u>	w<u>ay</u>	d<u>oor</u>	w<u>on't</u>	h<u>ead</u>

The final part of this activity is the transfer step—how we use rhyming words to read and spell other words. Begin the transfer part of this activity by telling children something like:

> "You know that when you are reading books and writing stories, there are words you have never seen before. You have to figure them out. One way people figure out how to read and spell new words is to see if they already know any rhyming words or words that have the same spelling pattern. I am going to write some words and you can see which words with the same spelling pattern will help you read them. Then, we are going to spell some words by deciding which words they rhyme with."

Write two or three words that rhyme and have the same spelling pattern as the words in the pocket chart. Let the children underline the spelling pattern and put each word in the pocket chart under the other words with the same spelling pattern. Help the children use the rhyme to decode the words.

Finally, say two or three words that rhyme. The children decide what words they rhyme with and use the spelling pattern to spell them. Here are the *I Wish That I Had Duck Feet* words along with the new words read and spelled based on their rhymes and spelling patterns.

wh<u>y</u>	br<u>own</u>	pl<u>ay</u>	fl<u>oor</u>	d<u>on't</u>	inst<u>ead</u>
dr<u>y</u>	t<u>own</u>	w<u>ay</u>	d<u>oor</u>	w<u>on't</u>	h<u>ead</u>
sk<u>y</u>	cl<u>own</u>	tr<u>ay</u>	p<u>oor</u>		br<u>ead</u>

Any book with lots of rhyming words—most of which have the same pattern—is a good candidate for a Rounding Up the Rhymes lesson. Because you will only round up the rhymes from part of the book, you can choose pages on which most of the rhymes have the same spelling pattern. You don't want to throw out more words than you keep! Many teachers tie this activity in with an author study of Dr. Seuss. Some of his other books that work particularly well are *In a People House, Ten Apples Up on Top,* and *One Fish, Two Fish, Red Fish, Blue Fish.* Other great books for Rounding Up the Rhymes include:

Golden Bear, by Ruth Young (Scholastic, 1992)
How I Spent My Summer Vacation, by Mark Teague (Crown, 1995)
Inside, Outside Christmas, by Robin Spowart (Holiday House, 1998)
Penguins Climb, Penguins Rhyme, by Bruce McMillan (Harcourt Brace, 1995)
This Is the Pumpkin, by Abby Levine (Whitman, 1998)
Ten Little Dinosaurs, by Pattie Schnetzler (Accord, 1996)

MAKING WORDS

Making Words (Cunningham & Cunningham, 1992) is an activity in which children are given some letters and use these letters to make words. They make little words and then bigger words until the final word is made. The final word—the secret word—always includes all the letters they have, and children are eager to figure out what the word is. After making words, they put the letter cards away, and the teacher leads them to sort the words into patterns. The final step is the transfer step, in which children use the rhyming patterns to decode and spell some new words. (The final step in Making Words is just like the final step in Rounding Up the Rhymes.)

Here is a sample Making Words lesson. The children have the vowels *a* and *i* and the consonants *c, h, n, p,* and *s.* In the pocket chart at the front of the room, the teacher has large cards with the same letters. Her cards, like the small letter cards used by the children, have the uppercase letter on one side and lowercase letter on the other side. The consonant letters are written in black and the two vowels are in red.

The teacher begins by making sure that each child has all the letters needed.

"What two vowels will we use to make words today?"

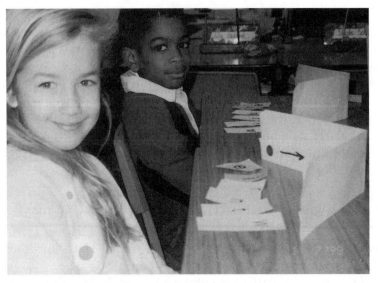

These children are ready to make words.

The children hold up their red *i* and *a* and respond appropriately.

The teacher has the children name the consonant letters, then writes a 3 on the board and says,

> "Let's begin with some 3-letter words. Take three letters and make *nap*. Everyone say *nap*."

The children quickly spell *nap* in their holders, and one child who has it made correctly is tapped to go and spell *nap* with the pocket-chart letters. The teacher puts the index card with the word *nap* in the pocket chart. Next she says,

> "Just change your vowel and you can change *nap* to *nip*. Everyone say *nip*. A little dog will nip at your shoes."

The children make *nip* and then make four more 3-letter words: *sip, sap, pin,* and *pan*.

The teacher erases the 3 and writes a 4 on the board, then tells them to add just one letter to *pan* and they can make the word *span*. Because this word is unfamiliar to some children, the teacher explains that the part of a bridge that goes over the river is called the span. (If no connection can be made for this word, the teacher would just eliminate it from the lesson.)

"We say that the bridge spans the river. We also talk about how long an animal lives by calling it the life span. The average life span of a dog is about 12 years."

Next they change one letter to change *span* to *spin*. At this point, the teacher says,

"Don't take any letters out and don't add any. Just change where the letters are and you can change *spin* into *snip*."

They then make two more 4-letter words, *snap* and *pain*.

The teacher erases the 4 and writes a 5, and they use five of their letters to make the word *Spain*. The teacher ends the word-making part of the lesson as she always does by asking,

"Has anyone figured out the secret word—the word that can be made with all the letters? If you know, make that word in your holder and I will come and see what you have."

The teacher walks around and finds two children who have figured out the secret word. "This was a hard secret word today," she says as she sends both children to the pocket chart, and jointly they manipulate all the letters to make the big word. As they get almost to the end, the other children realize what the word is. They shout in amazement:

"It's spinach!"

Several children make faces—presumably because spinach is not their favorite food—and then they all make *spinach* in their holders.

After all the children have *spinach* made in their holders, the teacher has them close their holders, and together they read all the words they have made, which are lined up in the pocket chart:

nap	span	Spain
nip	spin	spinach
sip	snip	
sap	snap	
pin	pain	
pan		

The children know that after making words, they sort these words into patterns and then use these words to read and spell other words. The patterns they sort for include beginning letters, endings (*s*, *ed*, *ing*, *er*, *est*), and rhyming words. Today's lesson includes only words that begin with *s*, *p*, *n*, *sp*, or *sn*. The teacher has them sort the words according to the beginning

Words made in a Making Words lesson in which the secret word was Martin.

The secret word made with the big pocket-chart letters and in one of the children's holders.

letters, which the children know are all the letters up to the vowel. The words sorted for beginning letters look like this:

nap	sip	pan	span	snap
nip	sap	pin	spin	snip
		pain	Spain	
			spinach	

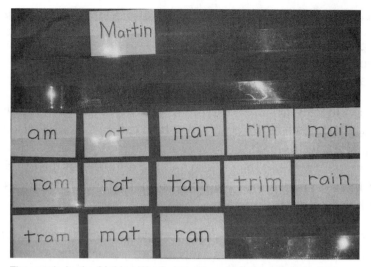

The words in the Making Words lesson sorted according to rhymes.

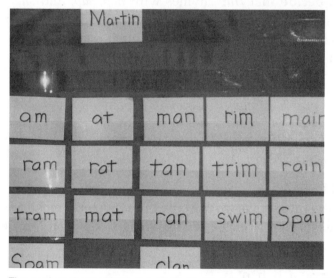

The pocket chart at the end of the Making Words lesson with the transfer words *Spam*, *clan*, *swim*, and *Spain*.

The teacher helps the children notice the beginning sounds and particularly the sound of *sp* and *sn* blended together at the beginning of words.

The next sort is for the rhyming words. The teacher asks:

"Who can come and find some rhyming words that will help us spell and read other words?"

Several children come up, and the words sorted into rhymes look like this:

nap	nip	pin	pan	pain
sap	sip	spin	span	Spain
snap	snip			

When the rhymes are sorted out, the teacher writes on index cards a few new words such as *flip* and *twin,* which can be decoded based on these rhymes. The children put the new words under the words with the same spelling pattern and use the pattern and the rhyme to figure out the words. Finally, the teacher reminds the children that thinking of rhymes can help them when they are writing too.

"What if you were writing and you wanted to write, *We set a trap to catch the mouse in our house.* How would you spell *trap*?"

The children decide that *trap* rhymes with *nap, sap,* and *snap* and will probably be spelled t-r-a-p. *Trap* is written on an index card and put with its rhyming counterparts. A similar procedure is used to decide that *brain* rhymes with *pain* and *Spain* and is probably spelled b-r-a-i-n. Here are the rhymes and transfer words in the pocket chart at the end of the lesson:

nap	nip	pin	pan	pain
sap	sip	spin	span	Spain
snap	snip	twin		brain
trap	flip			

One-Vowel Lessons

For the first several lessons, we use only one vowel. We make fewer words and have the children stretch out each word to develop their phonemic awareness.

Letters:	a d h n s
Make:	an and Dan has had sad sand hand hands
Sort for:	s h -ad -an -and
Transfer Words:	tan land mad glad

Letters:	e d n p s
Make:	Ed Ned den pen pens dens sped send spend
Sort for:	d s p -en -ed -end
Transfer Words:	ten fed bend sled

Letters:	i l p s t
Make:	is it sit pit tip sip lip slip spit split

Sort for: s -it -ip
Transfer Words: zip fit hit trip

Letters: o g n r s t
Make: go so no on Ron not rot rots song strong
Sort for: s r -o -on -ot -ong
Transfer Words: long hot lot trot

Steps in Planning a *Making Words* Lesson

1. Decide upon a "secret word" which can be made with all the letters. In choosing this word, consider child interest, the curriculum tie-ins you can make, and the letter/sound patterns to which you can draw children's attention through the sorting at the end.

2. Make a list of other words that can be made from these letters.

3. From all the words you could make, pick 12–15 words using these criteria:

   • Words that you can sort for the pattern you want to emphasize.

   • Little words and big words so that the lesson is a multilevel lesson (Making the little words helps your struggling students; making the big words challenges your highest-achieving students).

   • "Abracadabra" words that can be made with the same letters in different places (**side/dies**) so children are reminded that, when words are spelled, the order of the letters is crucial.

   • A proper name or two to remind students to use capital letters.

   • Words that most students have in their listening vocabularies.

4. Write all the words on index cards and order them from shortest to longest.

5. Once you have the two-letter, three-letter, etc., words together, order them so you can emphasize letter patterns and show how changing the position of the letters, changing one letter, or adding one letter results in a different word.

6. Choose some letters or patterns by which to sort.

7. Choose four transfer words—uncommon words you can read and spell based on the rhyming words.

8. Store the cards in an envelope. On the envelope, write the words in order, the patterns for which you will sort, and the transfer words.

From *Month-by-Month Phonics for Third Grade.* (Cunningham & Hall, 1998)
Material appears courtesy of Carson-Dellosa Publishing Company, Inc.

Letters: u b c r s

Make: us bus sub cub rub rubs cubs curb
curbs/scrub (2 secret words)

Sort for: c s r -us -ub

Transfer Words: tub Gus stub club

Unit-Connected Lessons

Many teachers pick the secret word from their science or social studies topics. Here are some lessons that go along with a science unit on energy.

Letters: e e i i c c l r t t y

Make: cry try ice rice city title elect cycle circle icicle
recycle tricycle electric electricity

Sort for: related words: electric, electricity; ice, icicle; cycle, recycle, tricycle

words ending in le: title, cycle, circle, icicle, recycle, tricycle

rhyming words: cry, try; ice, rice

Transfer Words: reply twice spry slice

Letters: a e e i b r s t t

Make: art/rat rate east beast/baste taste/state better
batter bitter rebate artist treaties batteries

Sort for: related words: art, artist
words in which y changed to i and added es:
batteries, treaties

rhyming words: rate, state, rebate
east, beast; baste, taste

Transfer Words: debate least paste feast

Letters: a e i c g m n t

Make: eat act age cage came game tame/team magic
manic anemic eating acting magnet magnetic

Sort for: related words: act, acting; eat, eating;
magnet, magnetic

words ending in ic: magic, manic, anemic, magnetic
rhyming words: age, cage
                             game, name, tame

Transfer Words: became stage shame rage

Lessons With "Cool" Secret Words

It is fun to teach some Making Words lessons in which the secret word is the name of a food, car, famous personality, or other "cool" word. Here are three lessons connected to some favorite foods.

Letters: e i c k n r s s

Make: in ski ice nice rice rink sink/skin sick rise risen/rinse skier sicken Snickers

Sort for: related words: ski, skier; rise, risen; sick, sicken

         rhyming words: in, skin
                                ice, nice, rice; rink, sink

Transfer Words: advice Berlin shrink price

Letters: e e i o c h r s

Make: is his rich hero echo core score shore chore cheer sheer heroes echoes riches Cheerios

Sort for: related words: hero, heroes; echo, echoes; rich, riches (es ending)

         rhyming words: core, score, shore, chore
                                cheer, sheer; is, his

Transfer Words: reindeer adore restore steer

Letters: e e l r p s t z

Make: set pet pets/step/pest rest zest steep sleep slept reset spree pester seltzer pretzels

Sort for: related words: set, reset; pest, pester; sleep, slept

         rhyming words: set, pet, reset
                                pest, rest, zest
                                steep, sleep

Transfer Words: request invest upset jeep

Steps in Teaching a Making Words Lesson

1. Place the large letter cards needed in a pocket chart or along the chalk tray.
2. Have children pass out letters or pick up the letters needed.
3. Hold up and name the letters on the large letter cards and have the children hold up their matching small letter cards.
4. Write the number 2 (or 3 if there are no two-letter words in this lesson) on the board. Tell them to take two letters and make the first word. Have them say the word after you, stretching out the word to hear all the sounds.
5. Have a child who has the first word made correctly make the same word with the large letter cards on the chalk tray or pocket chart. Do not wait for everyone to make the word before sending someone to make the word with the big letters. Encourage anyone who didn't make the word correctly at first to fix the word when they see it made correctly.
6. Continue to make words, giving students clues such as "Change just the first letter" or "Move the same letters around and you can make a different word" or "Take all your letters out and make another word." Send a child who has the word made correctly to make that word with the large letter cards. Cue them when they need to use more letters by changing the number on the board to indicate the number of letters needed.
7. Before telling them the last word, ask, "Has anyone figured out the secret word we can make with all our letters?" If so, congratulate them and have them make it. If not, say something like, "I love it when I can stump you." Give them clues to help them figure out the big word.
8. Once all the words have been made, take the index cards on which you wrote the words and place them one at a time (in the order made) in the pocket chart or along the chalk tray. Have the children say and spell the words with you as you do this. Use these words for sorting and pointing out patterns. Pick a word and point out a particular spelling pattern—beginning letters, endings, related words, and rhymes. Ask children to find the others with that same pattern. Line these words up so that the pattern is visible.
9. To encourage transfer to reading and writing, show students how rhyming words can help them decode and spell other words. Write two words on index cards and have students put these two new words with the rhyming words and use the rhyming words to decode them. Finally, say two words that rhyme, and have students spell these words by deciding which words they rhyme with.

10. If you like, give them a take-home sheet with the same letters across the top (alphabetical order, vowels then consonants, so as not to reveal the secret word to parents). Have the children write capitals on the back, cut the letters apart, and make words to fill the boxes, including words made in class and others they can think of. Here is a sample for a lesson in which the secret word is Michael.

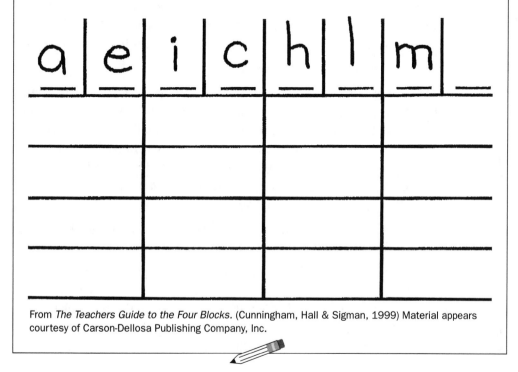

From *The Teachers Guide to the Four Blocks.* (Cunningham, Hall & Sigman, 1999) Material appears courtesy of Carson-Dellosa Publishing Company, Inc.

USING WORDS YOU KNOW

Another activity that helps children learn patterns and how patterns help you read and write is called Using Words You Know. To plan a Using Words You Know lesson, we pick three or four words that our children can read and spell and that have many rhyming words spelled the same way. While about half the word-wall words are irregular words such as *they*, *was*, and *have*, other words follow the expected pattern. Many teachers put a star on those word-wall words such as *big*, *play*, *not*, *make*, *ride*, and *thing* that help you spell lots of other words and use these in a Using Words You Know activity. Recently we have begun using some well-known brand names that have lots of rhyming words. We bring in packages with the product names and then use those names as the known words. Children are highly motivated by these products and are fascinated to see how many other words these products can help them read and spell. Here is a sample lesson using ice cream and Cool Whip.

We begin the lesson by displaying the products and letting children talk a little about them. Next we draw their attention to the names and tell them that these names will help them spell and read a lot of other words. Using the board, chart, or overhead, we make columns and head each with one of the key words, underlining the spelling pattern. The students do the same on a sheet of paper. At the beginning of the lesson, their papers look like this:

ice   cr<u>eam</u>   c<u>ool</u>   wh<u>ip</u>

We then show them words that rhyme with *ice, cream, cool,* or *whip*. We do not say these words and do not allow them to say the words but rather have them write them in the column with the same spelling pattern. We send one child to write the word on the chart, board, or overhead. When everyone has the word written under the word that will help them read it, we have them say the known word and the rhyming word. We help them to verbalize the strategy they are using by saying something like,

"If c-r-e-a-m is *cream,* d-r-e-a-m must be *dream.* If c-o-o-l is *cool,* d-r-o-o-l is *drool."*

After showing them 8–10 words and having them use the known word to decode them, we help them practice using known words to spell unknown words. To help them spell, we can't show them a word. Rather, we say a word, such as "twice," and have them say the word and write it under the word that it rhymes with. Again, we help them verbalize their strategy by leading them to explain,

"If *ice* is spelled i-c-e, *twice* is probably spelled t-w-i-c-e. If *whip* is spelled w-h-i-p, *strip* is probably spelled s-t-r-i-p."

Here are what the children's sheets might look like when all the one-syllable rhyming words have been added:

<u>ice</u>	cr<u>eam</u>	c<u>ool</u>	wh<u>ip</u>
nice	dream	drool	tip
mice	stream	pool	skip
slice	scream	fool	trip
twice	gleam	spool	strip
dice	beam	stool	clip

To make the lesson a bit more multilevel and show children that decoding and spelling based on rhyming words works for bigger words too, we would end the lesson by showing them a few longer words and having them write them under the rhymes and use the rhymes to decode them. Finally, we would say a few longer words, help them with the spelling of the first syllables, and have them use the rhyme to spell the last syllable. Here is what their papers would look like with some added longer words:

ice	cream	cool	whip
nice	dream	drool	tip
mice	stream	pool	skip
slice	scream	fool	trip
twice	gleam	spool	strip
dice	beam	stool	clip
sacrifice	mainstream	whirlpool	equip
device	downstream	preschool	spaceship

It is very important for Using Words You Know lessons (and the transfer step of Rounding Up the Rhymes and Making Words lessons) that you choose the rhyming words for them to read and spell rather than ask them for rhyming words. In English, there are often two spelling patterns for the same rhyme. If you ask them what rhymes with *cream*, or *cool*, they may come up with words with the e-e-m pattern such as *seem* and words with the u-l-e pattern such as *rule*. The fact that there are two common patterns for many rhymes does not hinder us while reading. When we see the word *drool*, our brain thinks of other o-o-l words such as *cool* and *school*. We make this new word *drool* rhyme with *cool* and *school* and then check out this pronunciation with the meaning of whatever we are reading. If we were going to write the word *drool* for the first time, we wouldn't know for sure which spelling pattern to use, and we might think of the rhyming word *rule* and use that pattern. Spelling requires both a sense of word patterns and a visual checking sense. When you write a word and then think, "That doesn't look right!" and then write it using a different pattern, you are demonstrating that you have developed a visual checking sense. Once children become good at spelling by pattern—rather than putting down one letter for each sound, we help them develop their visual checking sense through two activities: Reading/Writing Rhymes and What Looks Right? During Using Words You Know lessons, we are trying to get them to spell based on pattern, and we "finesse" the problem of two patterns by choosing the words we present to them.

Using Words You Know lessons are easy to plan if you use a good rhyming dictionary. We use the *Scholastic Rhyming Dictionary* (Young, 1994).

Children enjoy Using Words You Know, especially if the words you use are popular products such as *Coke, Crest, Tang,* and *Cat Chow.*

Steps in Teaching a Using Words You Know Lesson

1. Display and talk about the words they know.
2. Make as many columns as needed on the board and on student papers. Head these with the known word and underline the spelling pattern.
3. Show one-syllable words written on index cards. Have them write them under the word with the same pattern and use the rhyme to pronounce the words.
4. Say one-syllable words and have them decide how to spell them by deciding which word they rhyme with.
5. Repeat the above procedure with longer words.
6. Help students explain how words they know help them read and spell lots of other words, including longer words.

Here are some sample lessons using popular products and places.

Products: B<u>old</u>   Sh<u>out</u>   Ch<u>eer</u>

One-syllable words to read: sold, scout, told, deer, mold, shout, clout, trout, peer, steer

One-syllable words to spell: gold, pout, spout, sprout, jeer, sneer, cold, scold, stout, fold

Longer words to read: checkout, reindeer, blackout, blindfold, scaffold, knockout, uphold, dropout, engineer

Longer words to spell: cookout, without, household, handout, unfold, fallout, withhold, pioneer, volunteer

Products: K<u>it</u> Kat   Go<u>ld</u> F<u>ish</u>

One-syllable words to read: spit, split, that, grit, flat, dish, bold, spat, mold, rat

One-syllable words to spell: slit, old, hold, wish, swish, quit, chat, hat, hit, brat

Longer words to read: admit, profit, misfit, wildcat, credit, democrat, selfish, unselfish, acrobat, blindfold

Longer words to spell: permit, visit, combat, outfit, nonfat, catfish, starfish, billfold, doormat

Products: K<u>oo</u>l A<u>i</u>d   P<u>o</u>p C<u>or</u>n

One-syllable words to read: horn, cop, raid, worn, drop, maid, prop, fool, shop, born

One-syllable words to spell: torn, flop, braid, scorn, crop, thorn, tool, stool, paid, chop

Longer words to read: mermaid, lollipop, unicorn, stillborn, workshop, bridesmaid, prepaid, toadstool

Longer words to spell: newborn, unpaid, raindrop, gumdrop, acorn, afraid, nonstop, stepstool

Places: Taco B<u>ell</u>   Burger K<u>ing</u>   Pizza H<u>ut</u>

One-syllable words to read: fell, part, shut, bring, yell, sting, string, shell, sell, rut, quell, fling

One-syllable words to spell: ring, spring, swell, wing, swing, smell, strut, glut, spell, well

Longer words to read: haircut, misspell, firststring, darling, inning, peanut, dumbbell

Longer words to spell: retell, shortcut, seashell, something, hamstring, upswing, undercut

WORD SORTING AND HUNTING

Word Sorts (Henderson, 1990) have long been advocated as an activity to help children know what to attend to, and to develop the habit of analyzing words to look for patterns. There are a variety of ways to do Word Sorts, but the basic principles are the same. Children look at words and sort them into categories based on spelling patterns and sound. Children say the words and look at how they are spelled. They learn that to go in a certain category, the words must "sound the same and look the same." After sorting words chosen by the teacher, children hunt for other words in books, magazines, and other print around them and then sort these additional words for the patterns as well. In word hunts, teachers help students identify the patterns and then direct children to locate those patterns as they occur naturally in other print sources.

In many classes, different groups of children are working on different levels of sorts. Many teachers do a directed sorting lesson with a group of children first, and then the children continue sorting and hunting in their groups or in partner formats. Here is one example of how one teacher manages several different levels of spellers using a variety of sorting formats.

The teacher is meeting with a group of children who need to work with the various spellings of the vowel *a*. She has divided a transparency into four columns, and the children have all divided their papers into four columns. The teacher heads each column with a vowel pattern and a word the children know that has that pattern. The children set up their columns just like those on the transparency. Question marks are put in the last column to indicate the place to put other words with *a* that don't fit in the first three columns.

a	ai	a-e	???
<u>cat</u>	<u>rain</u>	<u>make</u>	<u>are</u>

As children write each word, the teacher helps them focus on the sound of the *a* and the spelling. *Cat* has just an *a* and the *a* says *a* like in *apple*. *Rain* has an *ai* and is pronounced like *ape*. *Make* is spelled with an *a*, a consonant letter, and an *e*, and the *a* is also pronounced like *ape*. *Are* looks like *make* but does not sound like *make*, so it heads the ??? column. The teacher then shows children words with *a* and has them read each word and decide which column it goes in. To go in a column, it must both look the same and sound the same. The first four words the children see and pronounce are: *map*, *name*, *paid*, and *pad*. The children pronounce them, stretching out the sound of the vowel, and write them in the appropriate column, and the teacher writes them in the column on the transparency:

a	ai	a-e	???
<u>cat</u>	<u>rain</u>	<u>make</u>	<u>are</u>
map	paid	name	
pad			

The next word is *have*. The children want to immediately write it under *make*, but the teacher has them stretch it out, and they decide that it looks like *make* but sounds like *cat*. It has to go into the ??? column. The teacher continues showing them words containing the letter *a*, which they pronounce and then write in the correct column. They have some trouble with *taste* because there are two consonants between the vowels, but the teacher explains that the pattern is *a* and one or more consonants and the *e*, and they decide it can go with *make*. They decide that *saw* and *park* have to go in the ??? column along with *was*. Here is what their papers and the transparency look like when 15 words have been sorted.

a	ai	a-e	???
<u>cat</u>	<u>rain</u>	<u>make</u>	<u>are</u>
map	paid	name	have
pad	wait	taste	saw

fast	brain	rate	park
jazz		safe	was

On the following day, this group works by themselves. One member of the group is the leader and gets to "play teacher." He shows each word (on index cards prepared by the teacher), has the group pronounce the word, and then writes it on the transparency after the group members have written it on their sheets. If there is disagreement on which column a word should go in, the leader does not write it anywhere but puts it aside to ask the teacher about when the teacher returns to check their work. At the end of this second day, their papers and the transparency looks like this:

a	ai	a-e	???
cat	rain	make	are
map	paid	name	have
pad	wait	taste	saw
fast	brain	rate	park
jazz	jail	safe	was
lamp	main	crane	Paul
crash	fail	date	want
brag	bait	case	
pant	drain	place	

Meanwhile, on the second day, while this group is working on their own with a "play teacher," the real teacher is doing a Word Sort introduction with a group of children who are working with spelling changes when *s* is added to words. This group's papers and transparency have these three columns:

s	es	ies
cats	churches	babies

Working with this group, the teacher shows them words, which they pronounce and then write in the appropriate column. At the end of the first day, their columns look like this:

s	es	ies
cats	churches	babies
animals	boxes	ladies
whales	lunches	puppies
crabs	branches	berries
cameras	ashes	parties
cars	taxes	countries

The only word that is difficult for this group is *whales*. Some children think it should go in the "es" column because it ends with *es*, but they decide that what you are focusing on was what was added, and since the word *whale* ends in *e*, only the *s* was added.

On the next day, the group working with *a* works with partners to find more words with *a* for their group to sort on the fourth day. Each set of partners is given 10 index cards and told to find "10 terrific words with *a*." They write the word they find in big letters on one side of the card, and then, on the other side, they print the key word (in teeny letters) to show what column they think it goes in. Meanwhile, the *s, es, ies* group is doing their "play teacher day," and the real teacher is doing a sort introduction with another group of students who are sorting words with vowels followed by *r* into these columns:

ar	or	er	ir	ur	???
car	for	her	bird	curl	work

After sorting with the teacher today, this group will work in a "play teacher" group on the second day, and then work with partners on the third day to find "ten terrific words" and write them on index cards for their group to sort on the fourth day.

Children in every grade are at all different levels in their spelling abilities. Teachers who are good "kid watchers" look at how children spell words in their first-draft writing to decide what spelling patterns children are ready to learn. The arrangement just described shows how teachers might work children on a number of different spelling levels. In this classroom, the procedure for each group was:

Day 1. Teacher-directed introduction of a new sort.

Day 2. Group continues to sort words created by teacher under the direction of a "play teacher."

Day 3. Partners work together to find 10 terrific words for their group to sort tomorrow. Teacher checks their cards before their group convenes again.

Day 4. Group convenes and each partnership gets to "play teacher" by presenting their 10 terrific words to the group to be written in the correct columns.

Day 5. Children in group hunt for more words or choose words they really like for each pattern and copy them into a page in their spelling notebook, putting words in the correct columns.

Word sorting and hunting are wonderful activities to develop spelling and decoding skills because children are actively involved in discovering "how words work." Many teachers post charts with the categories the class has worked on, and children are encouraged to add words that fit the pattern any time they find them in anything they are reading. Some children keep word notebooks and add words they find that fit particular categories as they find them throughout the year. In classrooms in which word sorting and hunting are regular activities, children love meeting a "new word" and thinking about where it might fit in all the various categories they have worked on. Most children love collecting things—word sorting and hunting encourage word collecting! The best source for information about word sorting and hunting is *Words Their Way* (1996) by Donald Bear, Marcia Invernizzi, Shane Templeton, and Francine Johnston.

READING/WRITING RHYMES

Reading/Writing Rhymes is another activity that helps students learn to use patterns to decode and spell hundreds of words. In addition, all beginning letters (onsets) are reviewed every time you do a Reading/Writing Rhymes lesson. Once all the rhyming words are generated on a chart, students write rhymes using these words and then read each other's rhymes. Because writing and reading are connected to every lesson, students learn how to use these patterns as they actually read and write. Here is how we do Reading/Writing Rhymes lessons.

You will need an onset deck containing cards for all the beginning sounds. The cards, 3 X 5 index cards, are laminated and have the single letter consonants written in blue, the blends in red, and the digraphs and other two-letter combinations in green. On one side of each card, the first letter of the onset is a capital letter. The onset deck contains 50 beginning letter cards including:

Single consonants: b c d f g h j k l m n p r s t v w y z
Digraphs (two letters, one sound): sh ch wh th
Other two-letter, one-sound combinations: ph wr kn qu
Blends (beginning letters blended together, sometimes called clusters): bl br cl cr dr fl fr gl gr pl pr sc scr sk sl sm sn sp spr st str sw tr

At the beginning of the lesson, we distribute all the onset cards to the students. Depending on your class, you can distribute them to individual children or to teams of two or three children. Once all the onset cards are distributed, we write the spelling pattern we are working with 10–12 times on a piece of chart paper. As we write it each time, we have the children help spell it and pronounce it.

Next, we invite children who have a card that they think makes a word to come up and place their card next to one of the written spelling patterns and pronounce the word. If the word is indeed a real word, we use the word in a sentence and write that word on the chart. If the word is not a real word, we explain why we cannot write it on the chart. (If a word is a real word and does rhyme but has a different spelling pattern, such as *bread* to rhyme with *ed*, we explain that it rhymes but has a different pattern and include it on the bottom of the chart with an asterisk next to it.) We write names with capital letters, and if a word can be a name and not a name, such as Jack and jack, we write it both ways. When all the children who think they can spell words with their beginning letters and the spelling pattern have come up, we call children up to make the words not yet there by saying something like,

> "I think the person with the *sp* card could come up here and add *sp* to *ed* to make a word we know."

We try to include all the words that any of our children would have in their listening vocabulary but we avoid obscure words. If the patterns we wrote to begin our chart get made into complete words, we add as many more as needed. Finally, if we can think of some good longer words that rhyme and have that spelling pattern, we add them to the list. (We spell and write the whole word here, since children do not have the extra letters needed to spell it.)

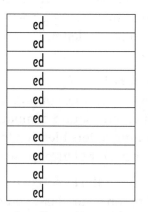

Chart for the *ed* spelling pattern as lesson begins.

Here is the completed *ed* chart.

Once the chart of rhyming words is written, we work together in a shared writing format to write a couple of sentences using lots of the rhyming words. Next the students write rhymes. Many teachers put the children in teams to write these rhymes and then let them read their rhymes to the class.

You can use the Reading/Writing Rhymes format to teach any of the common vowel patterns. If you are using a basal reader or curriculum guide that specifies an order in which the vowel sounds will be taught and tested, let that order determine the order in which you make charts for Reading/Writing Rhymes. Just as for Using Words You Know, we use a rhyming dictionary as our source for the rhyming words. We pick the patterns that have the most rhyming examples. (Some patterns will generate some "bad" words. You can either not distribute the beginning letters that would make those words, or tell children that there are some words that could be made which "we never use in school" so we won't include them. And you don't need anyone to tell you what they are!)

The next most common sounds vowels have are sometimes called the "long" sounds. Some children find it easier to figure out these long vowel words because you can actually hear the vowel "saying its name." Again, we don't want to confuse children by placing too much emphasis on the terminology or the rules. Rather, we want them to notice the pattern. The easiest and most consistent long vowel spelling for *a* is the a-y pattern, so we would begin with that one, using the same procedure of handing out all 50 beginning letter cards and inviting children who have

> Zack, Mack and Jack went
> inside for a snack. Jack and
> Mack ^were^ trying to lean over the crack
> with out falling on their back.
> Jack sat out back in the black
> shack looking in a crack for
> a snack. The geese ^sat^ on a crack
> out back then we came back and
> saw the geese leave and the track
> was black

Nathan and Edward's piece. Here is what two struggling readers wrote after helping the teacher create the chart of *ack* words. They took turns writing sentences—you can see the different handwriting. Notice also that almost all the other words are spelled correctly—a result of diligent daily word-wall practice, including on-the-back activities with endings and rhymes.

letters they think will make real words to come up and place their card next to the *ay* and say the word and put it in a sentence. When they have not noticed that their letters will make a word, we clue them by saying something like,

> "I think the person who has the *br* could come up here and spell the word that is the sound a donkey makes."

Just as we did for short vowels, we add longer *ay* words that rhyme at the end, along with any common rhyming words with a different spelling pattern. The children are always amazed at how many wonderful rhyming words there are on the *ay* chart and eagerly write lots of silly rhymes.

The second most common way of spelling the long vowel sound is to have an *a* followed by a consonant or two and then a silent *e*. A good way to introduce this is with the *ake* pattern because it has many appealing rhyming words. The other common combination for the long *a* sound is *a-i*. Many rhyming words can be spelled with *a-i* or *a-e*. The fact that

ay	
day	today
say	Monday
way	Tuesday
play	Wednesday
lay	Thursday
bay	Friday
hay	Saturday
may	Sunday
May	birthday
stay	away
stray	highway
clay	x-ray
gray	yesterday
pray	holiday
pay	faraway
way	subway
tray	*sleigh
Ray	*weigh
ray	*hey
sway	*they
slay	*ballet
bray	
spray	

The *ay* chart. The asterisk indicates words that rhyme
but have a different spelling pattern.

there are two common patterns is not a problem when reading. Students
quickly learn that both *a-i* and *a-e* often have the long *a* sound. When
spelling a word, however, there is no way to know which one is the correct spelling unless you recognize it as a word you know after writing it.
This is why we often write a word and then think, "That doesn't look
right," and then try writing it with the other pattern to see if that looks

ail	ale
sail	sale
tail	tale
trail	whale
snail	Dale
Gail	gale
hail	Yale
bail	stale
fail	scale
mail	male
frail	
pail	pale
wail	female
rail	tatteltale
quail	wholesale
nail	
jail	
detail	
monorail	
toenail	
cottontail	

Here is the chart for the *ail* and *ale* long-vowel spelling patterns.

right. When we write rhymes that have two common spelling patterns, we write both patterns on the same chart. Students come up and tell us the word their beginning letters will make, and we write it with the correct pattern. In many cases, there are two homophones, words that are spelled differently and have different meanings but the same pronunciation. We write both of these and talk about what each one means. Artistic teachers draw a little picture next to one of these so that students can tell them apart.

All the common vowel patterns can be taught through Reading/Writing Rhymes. We always choose the patterns that will generate the most

Here are the vowel patterns that are common enough to merit teaching and make good Reading/Writing Rhymes lessons:

For the short vowels, the most common rhyming patterns are:

ack	*ad*	*am*	*ap*	*ash*	*at*	*an*	*and*
ed	*et*	*est*	*ell*	*en*			
ick	*id*	*ip*	*ill*	*it*	*in*		
op	*ot*	*ock*	*ob*				
uck	*ug*	*ump*	*unk*	*ut*	*unch*		

Here are the long-vowel combinations that have the most examples:

ay   *ake*   *ail ale*   *ain ane*   *aid ade*   *ait ate*

eat eet   *eal eel*   *ead eed*

ice   *ide*   *ine*   *ite ight*

old   *o oe ow* (show)   *oke oak*   *ote oat*   *oan one*   *ute oot*

Some people consider the *ank, ang, ink, ing* patterns long vowels, and some people consider them short vowels. In many dialects, they are somewhere in between. In any case, they are common enough so that children should learn them.

ank   *ang*   *ink*   *ing*

The r-vowel patterns are:

ar   *ark*   *art*

are (care)   *air ear* (near)   *ear eer*

ert irt urt   *irl url*   *urn ern earn*

orn   *ort*   *ore oar*

The vowel *a* has special sounds when it is followed by *l, w,* or *u*:

aw   *all awl aul*

O is the vowel with the most different sounds:

ook   *ood*   *oom*   *ool*

oy   *oil*   *out*   *ow* (how)   *ew ue oo* (too)

rhymes, and when there is more than one common spelling for a rhyme, we include both, or in some cases all three spelling patterns.

WHAT LOOKS RIGHT?

What Looks Right? is an activity through which children learn that good spelling requires visual memory and how to use their visual memory for words along with a dictionary to determine the correct spelling of a word. In English, words that have the same spelling pattern usually rhyme. If you are reading and you come to the unknown words *plight* and *trite*, you can easily figure out their pronunciation by accessing the pronunciation associated with other *ight* or *ite* words you can read and spell. The fact that there are two common spelling patterns with the same pronunciation is not a problem when you are trying to read an un-familiar-in-print word, but it is a problem when you are trying to spell it. If you were writing and trying to spell *trite* or *plight*, they could as eas-ily be spelled t-r-i-g-h-t and p-l-i-t-e. The only way to know which is the correct spelling is to write it one way and see if it "looks right" or check your probable spelling in a dictionary. What Looks Right? is an activity to help children learn how to use these two important self-monitoring spelling strategies.

Here is a sample lesson for the *oat-ote* pattern. Using an overhead pro-jector or the board, create two columns and head each with an *oat-ote* word most of your children can both read and spell. Have the children set up two columns on their paper to match your model:

coat   vote

Have the children pronounce and spell the words, and lead them to real-ize that the words rhyme but have a different spelling pattern. Tell them that there are many words that rhyme with *coat* and *vote* and that you can't tell just by saying the words which spelling patterns they will have. Next say a word that rhymes with *coat* and *vote*, and write it both ways, saying, "If the word is spelled like *coat*, it will be g-o-a-t. If it is spelled like *vote*, it will be g-o-t-e." Write these two possible spellings under the ap-propriate word.

Tell the children to decide which one "looks right" to them and to write only the one they think is correct. As soon as each child decides which one looks right and writes it in the correct column, have each child use the dictionary to see if that spelling can be found. If the child cannot find the one that looked right, then have them look up the other possible spelling. Cross out the spelling you wrote that is not correct and continue with some more examples. For each word, again mention, "If it is spelled like *coat*, it will be g-o-a-t, but if it is spelled like *vote*, it will be g-o-t-e." Write the word both ways, and have each child write it the way it looks right and then look in the dictionary to see if the word is spelled the way the child thought.

Here is what your columns of words would look like after several examples:

coat	vote
goat	~~gote~~
boat	~~bote~~
float	~~flote~~
~~noat~~	note
~~quoat~~	quote
throat	~~throte~~
bloat	~~blote~~

To make your lesson more multileveled, include some longer words in which the last syllable rhymes with *coat* and *vote*. Proceed just as before to write the word both ways and have children choose the one that looks right, write that word, and look for it in the dictionary. For the *coat-vote* lesson, here are three longer words you might use:

~~promoat~~	promote
~~devoat~~	devote
~~remoat~~	remote

Here is a lesson for the *ait-ate* pattern. Notice that several of these pairs are both words. Children should find both *gate/gait* and *plate/plait*. This is an excellent time to talk about homophones and how the dictionary can help you decide which word to use. Also notice the words written at the bottom. Whenever we think of common words such as *great*, *eight*, *weight*, and *straight* that don't follow the pattern, we point these out to children, explaining that most—but not all—words that rhyme with *date* and *wait* are spelled a-t-e or a-i-t.

What Looks Right? is a versatile strategy and can be used to help children become better spellers of longer words. Here are two lessons for the *tion/sion* and *le/el/al* patterns.

While you are working with all these rhyming words is a wonderful time to have your children write some poetry. Select a poem or two your children will like, and read it to them several times. Then have them decide which words rhyme and whether or not the rhyming words have the same spelling patterns. Using these poems as models and the rhyming words you have collected as part of your spelling pattern lessons, students can write some interesting rhyming poetry.

date	wait
~~bate~~	bait
fate	~~fait~~
hate	~~hait~~
skate	~~skait~~
gate	gait
plate	plait
state	~~stait~~
rebate	~~rebait~~
debate	~~debait~~
donate	~~donait~~
hibernate	~~hibernait~~

**straight   eight   weight   great

motion	pension
action	~~acsion~~
station	~~stasion~~
~~maxtion~~	mansion
mention	~~mexsion~~

lotion	losion
nation	nasion
tention	tension
attention	attension
extention	extension
divition	division
multiplication	multiplicasion
television	television
vacation	vacasion
collition	collision

people	model	animal
travle	travel	traval
little	littel	littal
channle	channel	channal
locle	locel	local
equle	equel	equal
loyle	loyel	loyal
settle	settel	settal
poodle	poodel	poodal
bubble	bubbel	bubbal
tunnle	tunnel	tunnal
normle	normel	normal
generle	generel	general
possible	possibel	possibal
invisible	invisibel	invisibal
principle	principel	principal

COACHING FOR STRATEGIC DECODING AND SPELLING

A basic principle of *Phonics They Use* is that the work we do with words is only useful and worthwhile if children actually use what they know while reading and writing. In all word activities, we stress transfer to reading and writing. In Guess the Covered Word activities, we emphasize helping children verbalize how using meaning, all the beginning letters, and word length helps you make a very good guess. By ending each and every Making Words and Rounding Up the Rhymes lesson with a few transfer words that the rhyming words will help them read and spell, we are constantly reminding children how and when to use their word strategies. Children write using words used in Reading and Writing Rhymes and What Looks Right? lessons.

In spite of all this concerted effort, there are some obstinate children who "just don't get it!" They participate and seem to understand our word activities, but when they read and write, they don't use what they know. There are two ways to help children use more of what they know.

Coaching During Writing Conferences

Writing conferences provide an opportunity to coach children to use what we know they have learned about spelling. When we publish a book or prepare pieces for display on the bulletin board, we help children to spell the words correctly so that other people can read what they wrote. There are many words that children use in their writing which they can't be expected to know how to spell. When we are conferencing with them, we may simply acknowledge the good efforts shown in their attempts at spellings and then write the correct spelling. But at other times, we use the editing conference as the teachable moment to nudge them forward in their use of spelling patterns. Imagine that you are editing with a child, and the child has written the word *trade* as *trd*. Ask that child:

> "Where's your vowel? Every word needs at least one vowel. Remember in Making Words we always use at least one red letter in every word. Stretch out the word *trade* and listen for the vowel you hear."

The child will probably hear the *a.* Then help him decide where to put it. Add the *e* on the end and tell him that you can't hear the *e* but that if you say *trade* slowly, you can hear the *a,* and that when he is trying to spell a word to remember that every word needs at least one vowel.

Now imagine that another child comes to you with *trade* spelled *trad.* You might say something like:

> "That was a good try on *trade*. You wrote down every sound you heard. But let's look at the spelling pattern a-d. We know some a-d words. b-a-d spells *bad*; m-a-d spells *mad*; d-a-d spells *dad*. Can you think of a word that rhymes with *trade* and use that spelling pattern?"

If *made* is on the word wall, the child will probably realize that *trade* should be spelled with the same pattern. It is also possible (but not likely) that he will think of *paid* and want to spell *trade* t-r-a-i-d. In this case, point out that *trade* does rhyme with *paid* and could be spelled like *paid*, but point out the other pattern in words like *made* and *grade*.

Writing conferences are a great opportunity to individualize what we teach children. For some children, we just praise the invented spelling efforts and fix the spelling. For other children we use the opportunity to point out things about letters, sounds, and spelling patterns that they know when doing words but are not applying as they are writing.

Coaching During Reading

To coach children to use what they know while reading, we do some short (8–10 minutes) individual or very small group coaching sessions in which we lead them through the steps at the exact moment they need to use them. We use text that they haven't read before and that is going to contain some words they need to figure out. Having text at instructional level (5–10 errors per 100 words) is ideal. Explain to the children that the book will have words they haven't learned yet and that the purpose of these lessons is to practice how good readers figure out words they don't know. Have a child begin reading, and when the child comes to an unknown word and stops, say:

"Put your finger on the word and say all the letters."

Good readers look at all the letters in each word. Children who are struggling with reading tend to look quickly at the word, and if they don't instantly recognize it, they stop and wait for someone to tell them the word. Asking them to say all the letters forces them to look at all the letters. (Note, we are not giving the sounds of letters but rather naming the letters.) Sometimes, after saying all the letters, they correctly pronounce the word! This is proof that they aren't in the habit of looking at all the letters, and you should let them know what they have done by saying something like:

"That's right. There are lots of words we see when we are reading that we don't recognize right away, but when we look at all the letters, we can sometimes figure them out. Good job! Continue reading."

If, after saying the letters, the child does not say the word, you should say:

"Keep your finger on that word and finish the sentence."

It may seem foolish to have the child keep his or her finger there, but young children's print-tracking skills are not nearly as good as ours. Many children can't use the context of the sentence and the letters in the unknown word to figure out a word because once they get to the end of the sentence, they can't quickly look back and find the troublesome word. Keeping one finger on the word allows the child to quickly track back. If, after finishing the sentence, the child correctly pronounces the word, say something like:

> "Right. You can figure out lots of words you don't know if you use your finger to keep track of where the word is, finish the sentence, and then do like we do in Guess the Covered Word and guess a word that makes sense, begins with all the right letters, and is the right length. Continue reading."

If the child still does not get the word, you have three possible cues to point out. If there is a good picture clue (which the child has ignored), you could say,

> "What animal do you see in the picture that begins with *l*?"

If the troublesome word can be decoded based on one of the patterns on the word wall or used frequently during other word activities, you could say,

> "Let's see. The word is spelled s-t-r-i-n-g. We know that t-h-i-n-g spells *thing*. Can you make this word rhyme with *thing*?"

If there is nothing in the picture to help, and the word is not easily decodable based on a familiar rhyming word, you can give an explicit context clue. Imagine that the troublesome word is *place* in the sentence:

> *Clifford wanted to go to a far away place.*

You could say:

> "Where do you think Clifford might want to go that begins with p-l?"

If the child gets the word after you give the most appropriate cue, be sure to tell the child what he or she did.

> "Right. Lots of times there is something in the picture that matches a word we don't know, and if we use the picture and the letters and making sense, we can figure out the word."

Or:

> "Right. You can use words that rhyme with words you know to help
> you figure out lots of words, just the way we do on the back of our
> word-wall paper and when we figure out new words at the end of
> Making Words or Rounding Up the Rhymes."

Or:

> "Right. When you thought about where Clifford might go and the
> sound for the letters p-l, *place* was a word with all the beginning let-
> ters that made sense."

The tactics described so far will result in the reader figuring out an unknown word about 90 percent of the time. But there is always a word that
they still don't get, and if we tell them the word, we are reinforcing their
"wait and she will tell me eventually" decoding strategy. We never tell
them the word, but finally, when all else has failed, we will give them a
choice from which they can't fail to get the word. Imagine that the word is
ridiculous in the sentence:

> *That is a ridiculous hat.*

We say to the child:

> "Well, let's see. Do you think it says 'That is a ripe hat' or 'that is a
> ridiculous hat'?"

We make our alternative begin with the correct letters but be so unmean-
ingful that the child will make the right choice. We then say:

> "Good. That was a hard word but you got it! Let's continue reading."

Explaining this in writing makes it sound much longer and more com-
plicated than it actually is. When we are coaching a child to learn to use
what he or she knows (but isn't using), we choose text in which the child is
going to come to an unknown word every second or third sentence. When
the child stops at a word, we go through the following steps:

1. Put your finger on the word and say all the letters.
2. Keep your finger there and finish the sentence.
3. What do you see in the picture that starts with __?
   Or: Lets see, the word is spelled __. We can spell __. Can you make
      this rhyme with __?
   Or: Where do you think Clifford would go that starts with __?

4. Finally, if the cueing fails: "Let's see, do you think it says 'That is a ridiculous hat or that is a ripe hat'?"

When the child gets the word after any of our cueing, we congratulate the child and point out what strategy the child used that helped him or her figure out the word. If a child miscalls a word (instead of the usual struggling reader strategy of stopping on the word and waiting to be told), we wait for the child to finish the sentence. Then we repeat the sentence as the child read it, point out that it didn't make sense, and then take the child through as many steps as necessary.

Most children do not need the kind of one-on-one or very small group coaching described here, but for those who do, short coaching sessions held a few times each week make a world of difference in their ability to use what they know when they need to use it.

How All These Activities Are Multilevel

All the activities in this chapter have "something for everyone." Regardless of where your students are in their phonics and spelling abilities, there are things they can learn from each lesson format. Guess the Covered Word lessons provide continuous practice with all the beginning letter patterns. Children who already know most of their beginning letter sounds learn the important strategy of using meaning, all the beginning letters, and word length as cues to the identification of an unknown word.

Changing a Hen to a Fox provides practice with beginning, middle (vowel), and ending sounds. Children develop their phonemic awareness as they stretch out words and hear where in the word the letter needs to be changed. Children who know letter sounds see how these help them to spell lots of words. Changing a Hen to a Fox is a wonderful way to review letter-sound knowledge, particularly early in the year.

While Rounding Up the Rhymes, some children are still developing their phonemic awareness as they decide which words rhyme and are learning that rhyming words usually—but not always—have the same spelling pattern. As they use the words rounded up to read and spell new words, children who need it are getting practice with beginning letter substitution. Children who already have well-developed phonemic awareness and beginning letter knowledge are practicing the important strategy of using known words to decode and spell unknown rhyming words.

Making Words lessons are multilevel in a number of ways. Each lesson begins with short easy words and progresses to some medium-size and big words. Every Making Words lesson ends by the teacher asking,

"Has anyone figured out the word we can make if we use all our letters?" Figuring out the secret word that can be made from all the letters in the limited time available is a challenge to even our most advanced readers. Making Words includes even children with very limited literacy, who enjoy manipulating the letters and making the words even if they don't get them completely made until the word is made with the big pocket-chart letters. By ending each lesson with sorting the words into patterns and then using those patterns to read and spell some new words, we help children of all levels see how you can use the patterns you see in words to read and spell other words.

Using Words You Know lessons provide children who still need it with lots of practice with rhyming words and with the idea that spelling pattern and rhyme are connected. Depending on what they already know, some children realize how words they know can help them decode, while other children realize how these words help them spell. If you want to make the lesson a bit more multilevel at the upper end, include a few longer words that rhyme, and help students see how their known words can help them spell the rhyming part of longer words.

Word sorting and hunting are made multilevel by forming groups of children who indicate through their writing that they are ready to focus on particular patterns. The teacher then sets up a schedule so that different groups work with the teacher or together in cooperative formats on different days. The groups are not fixed but rather formed and re-formed as spelling needs and growth are evidenced.

Reading/Writing Rhymes and What Looks Right? are perhaps the most multilevel activities. All beginning letters, including the common single consonants and the less common, more complex digraphs and blends, are reviewed each time the teacher distributes the onset cards for Reading/Writing Rhymes. Phonemic awareness is developed as children say all the rhyming words and blend the vowel pattern with the beginning letters. Children whose word awareness is more sophisticated learn that there are often two spellings for the long-vowel patterns and develop their visual checking sense as they see the rhyming words with the different patterns. They also learn the correct spelling for many of the common homophones. The addition of some longer rhyming words helps them learn how to decode and spell longer words.

In What Looks Right? children learn to use the dictionary to check a possible spelling. They also learn how the dictionary can help you decide which way to spell a word when there are two words that sound the same but have different spellings and meanings.

ASSESSING PROGRESS

Good assessment is an ongoing activity. Teachers watch their children in a variety of reading and writing situations and notice what strategies the children are using and what they need to move them forward. In addition to the ongoing observations of children, which let us know what to teach that many children would profit from and are ready for, and what nudges particular children need, it is also good from time to time to stop and assess progress in a more systematic way. Remembering the principle "What they don't use, they don't have," we assess their decoding and spelling as they are actually reading and writing.

Observing Word Strategies in Reading

By observing children's reading, teachers can look at the misreadings children make and determine what word identification strategies they are using. Good readers will self-correct many of their misreadings. This usually indicates that they are using context to check that what they are reading makes sense. Successful self-correction is an excellent indicator that the reader is effectively using all three cueing systems: meaning (semantic), sounding-like language (syntactic), and letter-sound knowledge (graphophonic). Some readers tend to overuse context—their misreadings make sense but don't have most of the letter-sound relationships of the original word. Others overuse letter-sound knowledge. Their misreadings look and sound a lot like the original words, but they don't make any sense. By observing children's reading, we can determine what strategies they are using and what kind of instructional activities we might provide for them.

To look at children's word strategies while reading, we first must have something for them to read in which they make some errors—but not too many. This level is generally referred to as instructional level—the level of a book or story in which the child correctly identifies at least 90–95 percent of the words and has adequate comprehension of what was read. The text the child is reading should be something the child has not read before, and although the child may read more than 100 words, the first 100 words are generally used for analysis.

Teachers use a variety of materials to do this assessment—depending on what is available and what the school system requires. Some teachers use passages contained in the assessment package that accompanies many basal reading series. Other teachers or schools have designated certain "real" books as benchmark books. They don't use these books for instruction but only for assessment purposes. They decide that one book is what most children could read at the 90–95 percent word-identification accuracy level early in the year. Another book represents middle of grade difficulty level, and a third book is selected as end of grade level. In schools where Reading Recovery is used, some teachers use books designated by Reading-Recovery scoring to be at particular levels. Finally, some teachers use a published Informal Reading Inventory that contains graded passages beginning at preprimer level and going through sixth grade.

Regardless of what you use, the procedures are the same. You have the child read the text you think will be at instructional level. This text should be a text the child has not had a chance to read before. Tell the child that you cannot them while reading, and that when they get to a word they don't know, they should "do the best they can to figure it out" because you can't tell them any words. Also tell them that they should think about what they are reading because they will be asked to tell in their own words what the text they read was about after they read it.

As the child reads, we take an oral reading record. If we have made a copy of the text (or if we are using a passage from a basal assessment or an Informal Reading Inventory), we mark right on the passage. If not, we simply record on a sheet of paper. We use a simple marking system, and we only score the first 100 words.

> Put a check mark over each word read correctly.
>
> If the child misreads a word (*grows* for *growls*), write the error above it.
>
> If the child leaves a word out, circle that word.
>
> If the child self corrects, write **SC** above it. **SC** words are counted as correct.
>
> If the child makes the same error more than once, only count it one time.

After the child has read the passage, have the child close the book (or take the passage away) and ask the child to tell what the text was about. Ask questions as needed to determine that the child understood at least 70–80 percent of the information read. We consider passages in which the child's word-identification accuracy is in the 90–95 percent range and comprehension is at least 70–80 percent to be at the instructional level of the child. When we have recorded the oral reading of a child at instructional level, we can then analyze the child's misreadings and self-corrections to determine what word strategies the child is actually using.

Observing Word Strategies in Writing

Writing samples also show growth in word knowledge. Because writing results in a visible, external product, it is easier to determine what the children are actually using. By looking at two or three writing samples done a month or more apart, we can easily determine progress in word development. In looking at their writing sample to determine their level of word knowledge, we want to look at their spelling of high-frequency words and their attempts at spelling less-frequent words. First we notice whether all the word-wall words are spelled correctly. Next we look at how the child is spelling words on the wall and not readily available in the room. Do their invented spellings indicate that they can hear sounds in words and know what letters usually represent those sounds? Are the letters in the correct order? Are they beginning to spell by pattern rather than just putting down one letter for each sound? Are they using starred word-wall words to spell rhyming words? Are they adding endings correctly and beginning to use appropriate spelling changes?

In addition to writings on self-selected topics, many schools collect focused writing samples and look at these to determine growth in writing ability and word knowledge. A focused writing sample collected for assessment purposes should have a topic specified about which most children have good general knowledge, and children should write on this topic with no assistance from the teacher or any other child. Some examples of topics used in primary classrooms include:

My Favorite Things to Do
What I Like to Do at School
An Animal I Would Like to Have for a Pet

Many schools have the child write about the same topic at several different points in time—May of kindergarten, January and May of first grade, January and May of second grade, for example. These topic-focused nonassisted first drafts are then compared to determine an individual child's writing growth. In addition to a slew of valuable information about how the child writes—sentence sense, topic sense, word choice, writing conventions—these samples yield valuable information about the child's developing word knowledge.

Observing Word Strategies for Spelling Unknown Words

Here is another quick and simple measure we like to use to determine how children are developing their word knowledge. Making sure that each child cannot see what others are writing, we dictate 10 words to them which we don't expect them to be able to spell and then analyze their attempts. Teachers use a variety of words, the major criterion being that these words are not and have not been available in the room and that they show a variety of different patterns. Many teachers use the 10 words suggested by Gentry and Gillet on their Developmental Spelling Test (1993).

monster
united
dress
bottom
hiked
human
eagle
closed
bumped
type

(If your children like to write about monsters and thus have learned to spell *monster*, you might substitute another word, perhaps *blister* or *mountain*.)

Once children have spelled these words as best they can, Gentry and Gillet suggest analyzing their spelling using the following stages:

The Precommunicative Stage: Spelling at this stage contains scribbles, circles, and lines with a few letters thrown in at random. These letters usually are just there, and any connection between these letters and the words they are thinking is pure coincidence.

The Semiphonetic Stage: The second stage can be seen when words begin to be represented by a letter or two. The word *monster* may be written with just an *m* or an *mr* or a *mtr*. *Type* might be written with just a *t* or *tp*. This stage indicates that the child is beginning to understand letter-sound relationships and knows the consonant letters that represent some sounds.

The Phonetic Stage: In the third stage, vowels appear—not necessarily always the right vowels, but vowels are used and most sounds are represented by at least one letter. Phonetic spelling of *monster* might include *munstr* and *mostr*. *Type* will probably be spelled *tip*. You can usually tell when a child is in the phonetic stage because you can read most of what children in this stage write.

The Transitional Stage: In this stage, all sounds are represented and the spelling is usually a possible English spelling, just not the correct spelling. *Monster* in this stage might be spelled *monstir* or *monstur*. *Type* is probably spelled *tipe*.

The Conventional Stage: Finally, the child reaches the stage of conventional spelling, in which most words a child at that grade level could be expected to spell correctly are spelled correctly.

Of course, children's spelling of different words will indicate different stages. The important thing is not which stage they are in but how they are growing. Put the sample away along with writing samples and oral reading records, and use them to compare how they do on the very same tasks later in the year.

The Names Test

A final possibility to consider when assessing children's word knowledge is the Names Test. I developed the Names Test (Cunningham, 1990) several years ago when working with a group of older remedial readers. These boys were good context users, and it was quite difficult to determine what they knew about letter-sound patterns when they were reading contextually because they were such good context users. I wanted a measure of their word identification ability that was not confounded by context but that was not just a list of words. Reading a list of words is a rather "unnatural act," and choosing the words is quite difficult. If you choose words most children have in their listening vocabularies, you run the risk of also choosing words they know as sight words and thus don't have to decode, and you could overestimate their letter-sound knowledge. If you choose very obscure words, they probably don't have them in their listening vocabularies and thus can't use the "sounds right" clue to check their probable pronunciation. Nonsense words have the same problems. Nothing we ask kids to do is more unnatural than reading a list of made-up words (well, almost nothing!), and many children try to make the nonsense word into a word they have heard of; the nonsense-word test would thus be an underestimate of their decoding ability.

There is one type of word, however, that children hear often—and thus have in their listening vocabularies—but that they don't read often—and thus are not apt to have already learned as sight words.

Names are heard all over the place. Names are a big part of every TV and radio program, and usually these names are pronounced but not read. Names are one type of word that most children have a lot more of in their listening vocabularies than in their sight vocabularies; thus, I use names for the source of words to measure decoding ability not confounded by context.

In addition to their more-often-heard-than-read quality, names have another advantage for a word-reading test. We do sometimes read lists of names. Teachers and others often "call the roll"; thus, reading a list is a somewhat more natural real-reading task than most other word-list reading tasks. Here is the Names Test, with directions and suggestions for analyzing children's responses.

The Names Test of Decoding
(From Cunningham, 1990; additional names by F. A. Dufflemeyer.)

Jay Conway	Chuck Hoke
Kinberly Blake	Homer Preston
Cindy Sampson	Ginger Yale
Stanley Shaw	Glen Spencer
Flo Thornton	Grace Brewster
Ron Smitherman	Vance Middleton
Bernard Pendergraph	Floyd Sheldon
Austin Shepherd	Neal Wade
Joan Brooks	Thelma Rinehart
Tim Cornell	Yolanda Clark
Roberta Slade	Gus Quincy
Chester Wright	Patrick Tweed
Wendy Swain	Fred Sherwood
Dee Skidmore	Ned Westmoreland
Troy Whitlock	Zane Anderson
Shane Fletcher	Dean Bateman
Bertha Dale	Jake Murphy
Gene Loomis	

Procedures for Administering and Scoring the Names Test

(From Cunningham, 1990.)

Preparing the Instrument

1. Type or print the 35 names on a sheet of paper or card stock. Make sure the print size is appropriate for the age of the students being tested.
2. For students who might perceive reading an entire list of names as too formidable, type or print the names on index cards, so they can be read individually.
3. Prepare a protocol (scoring) sheet. Do this by typing the list of names in a column and following each name with a blank line to be used for recording a student's responses.

Administering the Names Test

1. Administer the Names Test individually in a quiet, distraction-free location.
2. Explain to the student that she or he is to pretend to be a teacher who must read a list of names of students in the class. Direct the student to read the names as if taking attendance.
3. Have the student read the entire list. Inform the student that you will not be able to help with difficult names, and encourage him or her to "make a guess if you are not sure."
4. Write a check on the protocol sheet for each name read correctly. Write phonetic spellings for names that are mispronounced.

Scoring and Interpreting the Names Test

1. Count a word correct if all syllables are pronounced correctly regardless of where the student places the accent. For example, either Yó/lan/da or Yo/lán/da would be acceptable.
2. For words in which the vowel pronunciation depends on which syllable the consonant is placed with, count them correct for either pronunciation. For example, either Ho/mer or Hom/er would be acceptable.
3. Count the number of names read correctly, and analyze those mispronounced, looking for patterns indicative of decoding strengths and weaknesses.

REFERENCES

Adams, M. J. (1990). *Beginning to read*. Cambridge, MA: MIT Press.

Bear, D. B., Invernizzi, M., Templeton, S., & Johnston, F. (1996). *Words their way: A developmental approach to phonics, spelling, and vocabulary, K–8*. New York: Macmillan/Merrill.

Cunningham, P. M. (1990). The names test: A quick assessment of decoding ability. *The Reading Teacher, 44*, 124–129.

Cunningham, P. M., & Cunningham, J. W. (1992). Making words: Enhancing the invented spelling-decoding connection. *The Reading Teacher, 46*, 106–107.

Cunningham, P. M., Hall, D. P., & Sigmon, C. M. (1999). *The teacher's guide to the four blocks*. Greensboro, NC: Carson-Dellosa.

Cunningham, P. M., & Hall, D. P. *Month by month phonics for third grade*.

Gentry, J. R., & Gillet, J. W. (1993). *Teaching kids to spell*. Portsmouth, NH: Heinemann.

Henderson, E. H. (1990). *Teaching spelling* (2d ed.). Boston: Houghton Mifflin.

Wylie, R. E., & Durrell, D. D. (1970). Teaching Vowels through Phonograms. *Elementary English, 47*, 787–791.

Young, S. *The Scholastic Rhyming Dictionary*. New York: Scholastic.

CHILDREN'S BOOKS CITED

(In addition to the books in the box on page 97, these were cited in the text.)

Tog the Dog (1986), *Jen the Hen* (1985), *Mig the Pig* (1984), and *Pat the Cat* (1993), by Colin and Jacqui Hawkins (Putnam).

Kinderrhymes—24 titles, including *Rimes with Cat, Rimes with Cap,* and *Rhymes with King* (Rigby, 1998).

Zoo Looking, by Mem Fox (Mondo, 1996).

Hatttie and the Fox, by Mem Fox (Simon and Schuster, 1988).

There's a Bug in My Mug, by Kent Salisbury (McClanahan, 1997).

My Nose Is a Hose, by Kent Salisbury (McClanahan, 1997).

I Wish That I Had Duck Feet, by Dr. Seuss (Random House, 1972).

4
BIG WORDS

Big words present special decoding problems for many readers. Most of the words we read are one-syllable words. Big words are less frequent, but they are the words that tell most of the story. Here is a paragraph from *Sports Illustrated for Kids* (July, 1989, p. 14) in which all the words of two or more syllables have been deleted and replaced with a blank:

Few things feel as good as _____ the _____ of your _____ _____ _____. You _____ the thrill of _____ him face to face, and you get to take home a _____ _____ .

As you can see, it is impossible to make sense of even simple paragraphs intended for children when you can't read any of the big words. Some of these big words are quite easy to decode because they consist of a one-syllable word with a common ending added or two common one-syllable words forming a compound word. The paragraph from the preceding example is now repeated with these easily decodable two-syllable words replaced:

Few things feel as good as __getting__ the _____ of your _____ __baseball__ __player__ . You _____ the thrill of __meeting__ him face to face, and you get to take home a _____ _____ .

You can now figure out that this paragraph is about baseball and has to do with meeting players, but you are still not getting much meaning from this paragraph. Here is the paragraph with all its words:

Few things feel as good as __getting__ the __autograph__ of your __favorite__ __baseball__ __player__ . You __experience__ the thrill of __meeting__ him face to face, and you get to take home a __valuable__ __memento__ .

Good readers could quickly decode these big words, but how do they do it? The strategy good readers appear to use is similar to the strategy used with one-syllable words. When faced with an unfamiliar-in-print big word, good readers search through their store of known words in order to find other words with the "same parts in the same places."

Autograph may be seen as "like *automobile* at the beginning and like *paragraph* at the end." *Favorite* may be seen as "beginning with *favor*, and then it has to be *favorite* to sound right in the sentence." *Experience* is more difficult for most children. They might decode it, however, by seeing that it begins like *experiment* and ends like *difference*. *Valuable* is *value* with the common suffix *able*. *Memento* is not too hard to decode, but many children might not have it in their listening vocabularies and might pronounce it with the first syllable accented—mee-men-to. If they know enough big words that end in *t-o*, such as *lotto* and *tomato* and *Pluto*, they will probably pronounce the last syllable correctly. If not, they will probably pronounce it like the known word *to*.

Once students reach the intermediate grades, they meet approximately 10,000 new words—words never before encountered in print—in their school reading each year (Nagy & Anderson, 1984). Most of these words are big words, words of seven or more letters and two or more syllables.

In spite of the importance of multisyllabic words, children are often given no instruction in decoding them. Historically, children were taught to use syllabication rules. After dividing the words into syllables, they were supposed to apply their phonics knowledge to the syllables. The syllabication rules were logical and well intended. Good readers do see polysyllabic words in chunks and they do know which syllable to accent, once they figure out the word. But good readers do not seem to do this by using rules (Canney & Schreiner, 1977). Rather, they look for chunks based on words they already know. Often—as in *autograph, favorite,* and *experience*—some chunks (*auto, favor, experi*) are larger than a syllable.

Traditionally, instruction in what was termed "structural analysis" was a part of most upper-elementary reading curriculums. This instruction usually included prefixes, suffixes, and Greek and Latin roots. These word parts were usually taught as clues for determining meanings for words, rather than as clues for pronouncing unfamiliar-in-print words. Often the word parts emphasized were parts with low utility. *Intra*, for example, was taught as a prefix meaning "within" with the examples of *intramural* and *intrastate*. According to the *American Heritage Dictionary*, 4th edition, 25 words begin with the letters *intra*. In most of these, such as *intractable*, the *in*, not the *intra*, is the prefix. Six words, including *intramural* and *intrastate*, begin with the prefix *intra*. The only other words students would be helped to figure out the meaning of from the prefix *intra* were *intravenous, intrauterine, intracellular,* and *intracellularity.* In addition to the lack of utility problem, many of the prefixes taught had as many examples in which the prefix did not add to the meaning of the word as those in which it did. *Mis* might help you figure out *misbehave* and *misdeal,* but it doesn't get you far with the meanings of *miscellaneous* and *mistletoe.*

Instruction about suffixes was often cluttered with grammatical jargon. The suffixes *ance* and *ence* were taught as changing the word from the verb form to the noun form and meaning "the condition or state of." It is doubtful that when students first encountered the word *difference,* they thought of the word *differ* (which is actually lower in frequency than *difference*) and then used *differ* to figure out a meaning for *difference*—"the condition or state of differing."

Finally, the usefulness of Greek and Latin roots is questionable. Shepard (1974) found that knowledge of Latin roots is not strongly related to knowledge of meanings of words, but that knowledge of stems that are current English words is strongly related to the meaning of related words. Many students know meanings for words such as *collect* and *receive* who don't know anything about the Latin roots *lect* and *ceive.* But students who know the word *sane* have little trouble with the less frequent related word *sanity.*

For a variety of reasons, this type of structural analysis is seldom found in upper-grade reading curricula today. Later in this chapter, when recommending instructional strategies to help children decode big words, the importance of morphological relationships will be highlighted, but it is important to note that the morphologically based instruction supported by research bears little resemblance to the rule-based, low-utility structural analysis done in the past.

In order to use known words to figure out big words, you must know some big words. Not only must you be able to read some big words, but you must also be able to spell those big words. You can't recognize *experience* as beginning like *experiment* and ending like *difference* unless you can both read and spell *experiment* and *difference.* The requirement that you be able to spell some big words along with the tendency of readers to guess or skip any word of more than seven letters may partially explain why so many older children experience problems reading their content-area texts.

This chapter will describe ways to help children build a store of big words they can read and spell and strategies for helping them use words they know to figure out unknown big words. In addition to big words from your content areas and big words of special interest to your students, you will learn about how some particularly helpful big words—the Nifty Thrifty Fifty—can unlock the spelling, decoding, and meaning of thousands of other words.

Big-Word Collectors

Kids love to collect things—sports cards, butterflies, shells, autographs. Teachers who want their students to be big-word experts can motivate their students by encouraging them to become big-word collectors! The collections can be both individual and classroom projects. Some collections can be permanent collections—needed for all kinds of reading and writing. Other collections can come and go as new topics, themes, and units are explored. Here are some of the ways teachers encourage big-word collecting.

Topic Word Boards

Reserve one of the bulletin boards in your room for use as a topic word board. Display some pictures related to the unit and tell students you need them to help you find big words needed to learn about the topic. Leave a supply of colored index cards next to the board, and as you and your students explore the unit, ask them for suggestions of topic-related words to add to the collection. When students suggest words, have them explain why that word is particularly important to the topic. Write words the class agrees belong in that collection with a black, thick permanent marker. Add words gradually and make sure the class agrees they are needed. Students who have input into the selection of the words to be learned have ownership and begin to see these words as "their words," not just "more words to learn."

As you and the students explore the topic, call attention occasionally to a word when it is used in discussion, reading, or other learning experiences. Help students to focus on the spelling of the words by having them chant the spelling (cheerleader style) with you. Then have them close their eyes and chant the spelling again. When you have a few minutes, challenge them to write a sentence that uses as many of the words as they can and still makes a sensible sentence. As students write about what they are learning, encourage them to use the words and to refer to the board for correct spellings. Help students to develop positive attitudes toward learning big words by pointing out that every field has some critical words, the use of which separates the pros from the amateurs.

When the unit is over and you begin another topic on this board, have different students write a personal meaning, an example sentence, and draw some kind of visual on the back of each card. Alphabetize these cards and place them in your collection. A file box arranged according to topic takes little space and is easily accessible by all. As the year goes on, your collection will grow to an impressive number. Encourage students to find a word in this box if they remember having used the word and need to find it later in the year. Take time occasionally to let students count words and use words across topics in a variety of word-sorting and categorizing activities. We all love looking at our collections from time to time, marveling at how they are growing and comparing old items with newly acquired ones.

Collect Big Words Needed for All Kinds of Reading and Writing

Another way to help students begin to notice and appreciate the power of words is to have them on the lookout for big words that "say it better." Focus on a word that you are tired of seeing in their writing and begin a chart for them to help you collect "Big Words for Said." Add a few that students suggest immediately and then add more gradually as students encounter them in their reading or discussions. For each word, have students give examples of sentences in which the word they want added would be a better word, and have the class as a whole decide if it is worth adding to the chart.

Weather

temperature climate
Satellites forecasting
prediction
thunderstorm hurricane
atmosphere tornado
latitude lightning pressure
longitude precipitation
snowfall
humidity rainfall
greenhouse moisture
weather vane blizzard
barometer rainbow
meteorologist typhoon

Topic word board for weather.

Washington, D. C.

Topic word board for Washington, D.C.

nation   government
president senators
Congress   Constitution
representatives federal
museum   Capital
monuments Capitol
national   sculpture
Congressional
tourists   embassies
demonstrations
inauguration

Add another chart after a few weeks and let children suggest words that should be added to both. In addition to collecting big words to replace "tired, overworked" words, this chart strategy also works well for having students be on the lookout and collect specific kinds of words such as compound words. Keep charts displayed as long as you can, given your limited classroom space, and then use the procedure described for Topic Boards to get meanings, examples, sentences, and visuals written on the back of each card and the cards filed according to category in some accessible way.

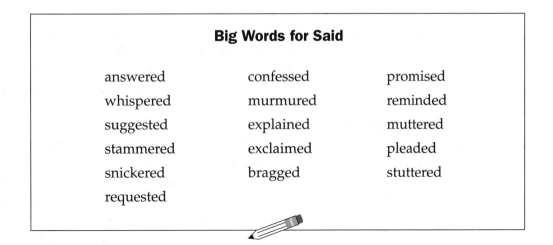

Big Words for Said

answered	confessed	promised
whispered	murmured	reminded
suggested	explained	muttered
stammered	exclaimed	pleaded
snickered	bragged	stuttered
requested		

Big Words Describing People

unhappy	curious	tremendous
delighted	famished	nervous
thrilled	patient	brilliant
overjoyed	miserable	mysterious
frightened	lovable	hilarious
paralyzed	astonished	

Compound Words

anybody	basketball	motorcycle	watermelon	downstairs	strawberry
jellyfish	everyone	woodpecker	applesauce	homework	football
birthday	keyboard	grandmother	toothbrush	rattlesnake	doorbell
boyfriend	headset	grasshopper	playground	starfish	rollerblade

Personal Collections

Once your students begin to understand the power of big words and how much fun it is to collect them, encourage them to start their own collections. Some teachers have students bring large, tabbed notebooks and label the different sections for topics of particular interest to each student. Other teachers provide small file boxes for each child, with dividers and 3 X 5 index cards. Children should establish categories they are interested in—baseball, computers, sea animals, Mexico, Disneyworld, scuba diving. As students find big words related to their categories, they write these on one side of the card and complete the card with a personal meaning, sentence example, and visual on the back, just as they do for the cards created for the class collections. (Children who don't like to draw love to find appropriate visuals on the web or in your clip-art collection! Encourage them to cut and paste.)

Once your students have begun their own big-word collections, give them time every few weeks to share the new words they have found and why these words are important to their topics. You may want to form small collecting groups, particularly if you have children with similar categories. Provide extra cards so that they can make extras to trade with their like-minded friends.

A wide vocabulary is one of the clearest indicators of intelligence, education, and literacy. Children who collect big words related to topics of interest to them increase their vocabularies in that area, and many of the words have meanings that carry over to other topics. Perhaps most important, their attitude towards big words changes. Instead of looking away and "skipping over" big new words, your students will approach big words with an "I wonder what it is. Maybe I need it" attitude that makes all the difference. Children who can read and spell some big words have the patterns to decode and spell lots of others. Regardless of the topic, children with personal big-word collections acquire facility and confidence with big words.

Here are some of the words one boy had in his basketball word collection. Notice how many of these words have application beyond the world of basketball and how many words have patterns applicable to other words.

technical	offensive	defensive	tournament	turnover	rebounds
coliseum	underdogs	referee	victorious	undefeated	semifinals
challenge	teammates	possession	contention	physical	dominate

RIVET—A VOCABULARY INTRODUCTION ACTIVITY

RIVET is an activity I created one day while sitting in the back of a fourth-grade classroom watching one of my student teachers trying to introduce some vocabulary words to her students. The vocabulary she was introducing was important to the story, and many students needed to focus on these words and their meanings. The student teacher was diligently writing the words on the board and having students use them in sentences and trying to help the students access meanings and relate them to each other. Unfortunately, the students were not particularly interested in the words, and their attention was marginal at best. When the words had been introduced and the students began to silently read the selection, I quietly approached some of the less able readers and helped them find the introduced words in their text and had them read the sentences containing these words to me. It was no surprise that for the children who didn't already know the pronunciation and meaning for these words, they hadn't learned them from the vocabulary introduction. RIVET was conceived that day and has since saved many a student teacher from the dreaded experience of having taught some words that no one seemed to have learned.

Activating children's prior knowledge and getting them to make predictions before they read is one sure way to increase the involvement and comprehension of most children. RIVET is an activity designed to accomplish this critical goal. To prepare for a RIVET text introduction, read the selection and pick six to eight important words—with a particular emphasis on big words and important names.

Begin the activity by writing numbers and drawing lines on the board to indicate how many letters each word has. Have the students draw the same number of lines on a piece of scratch paper. Your board and their paper at the beginning of the RIVET activity would look like this:

1. _ _ _ _ _ _ _ _ _ _
2. _ _ _ _ _ _ _ _
3. _ _ _ _ _ _ _ _
4. _ _ _ _ _ _ _ _
5. _ _ _ _ _ _   _ _ _ _ _ _ _ _
6. _ _ _ _ _ _ _ _
7. _ _ _ _ _ _ _ _ _

Fill in the letters to the first word one at a time, as the students watch. Encourage students to guess each word as soon as they think they know what it is. Most students could not guess the word when the board looks like this:

1. <u>u n e</u> _ _ _ _ _ _ _
2. _ _ _ _ _ _ _ _
3. _ _ _ _ _ _ _ _
4. _ _ _ _ _ _ _ _
5. _ _ _ _ _ _   _ _ _ _ _ _ _ _
6. _ _ _ _ _ _ _ _
7. _ _ _ _ _ _ _ _ _

But many will guess with a few more letters:

1. <u>u n</u> e x p e _ _ _ _

Once someone has guessed the correct word, ask him or her to help you finish spelling it and write it on the board as students write it on their papers. Begin writing the letters of the second word, pausing for just a second after writing each:

1. u n e x p e c t e d
2. a m _ _ _ _ _ _
3. _ _ _ _ _ _ _ _ _
4. _ _ _ _ _ _ _ _
5. _ _ _ _ _ _ _ _ _ _ _ _ _
6. _ _ _ _ _ _ _ _
7. _ _ _ _ _ _ _ _ _

The attention of all the students is generally riveted (thus the name RIVET) to each added letter, and with a few more letters many students will guess the word.

1. u n e x p e c t e d _ _
2. a m b u l _ _ _ _

If they are right, have them help you finish spelling it. If they give you an incorrect guess, just continue writing letters until someone guesses the correct word. Continue in this fashion until all the words have been completely written and correctly guessed. Here is what the board and student's papers would look like when all words were introduced:

1. u n e x p e c t e d
2. a m b u l a n c e
3. e m e r g e n c y
4. E l i z a b e t h
5. g o l d e n r e t r i e v e r
6. h u r r i c a n e
7. t e r r i f y i n g

Now have the students use these words to predict some of the events in the story. Encourage divergent predictions by asking questions that lead them to consider alternative possibilities. One child may say,

"A girl named Elizabeth was hurt in a hurricane."

Accept that response, but ask a question such as:

"Does Elizabeth have to be a girl character in the story?"

Help the students think about the fact that hurricanes are given names and perhaps this hurricane is named Elizabeth. Students may also realize that Elizabeth could be the golden retriever. Ask these kinds of questions even if the first prediction is correct. Prediction is a powerful activity, not because the predictions are always right, but because the process of predicting requires that students access whatever prior knowledge they have and bring it to bear on the selection. After the students have read the selection, use the key words to review their predictions and talk about what actually happened. Be sure to let the students know that you are not just interested in "the right answer." You may want to say something like, "That didn't happen, but it could have, and it might have made a more interesting story."

In addition to being a wonderful vocabulary introduction and prediction activity, RIVET focuses your students' attention on looking at all the letters of big words in sequence. Looking at all the letters in sequence is essential to learning how to decode and spell big words.

MODELING: HOW TO FIGURE OUT A BIG WORD

When you model, you show someone how to do something. In real life, we use modeling constantly to teach skills. We would not think of explaining how to ride a bike. Rather, we demonstrate and talk about what we are doing as the learner watches what we do and listens to our explanation. Vocabulary introduction is a good place to model for students how you figure out the pronunciation of a word. The word should be shown in a sentence context so that students are reminded that words must have the right letters in the right places and make sense. Following is an example of how you might model for students one way to decode *entertainment*:

> "I am going to write a sentence on the board that has a big word in it. I will 'think aloud' how I might figure out this one. After I show you how I decode this one, I will let several of you model how you would decode other words."
>
> Write on the board: *Different people like different kinds of entertainment.*
>
> "Now I am going to read up to the big word and tell you how I might figure it out. If you figure out the word before I do, please don't say it and ruin my performance!"
>
> Read the sentence and stop when you get to *entertainment*.
>
> "This is a long word, but I can probably figure it out if I think of some other words I know."
>
> Cover all but *enter*.
>
> "The first chunk is a word I know—*enter*. The second chunk is like container and maintain."
>
> Write *container* and *maintain* on the board, underlining the *tain*.

"Finally, I know the last chunk is like *argument* and *moment.*"

Write *argument* and *moment* on the board, underlining the *ment*.

"Now I will put the chunks together: *enter-tain-ment.* Yes, that's a word I know, and it makes sense in the sentence because my brother and I certainly are different and we don't like the same TV shows or movies or anything."

Since English is not a language in which letters or chunks have only one sound, you might also write the word *mountain* on the board, underlining the *tain* and pointing out to students that the letters *tain* also commonly have the sound you hear at the end of *mountain.* Have students try pronouncing *entertainment* with the different sounds for the *tain* chunk. Point out that it sounds right and makes a word you know when you use the sound of *tain* you know from *maintain* and *container.* Remind students that if they use the probable sound of letters together with the sense of what they are reading, they can figure out many more words than if they just pay attention to the letter sounds, ignoring what makes sense, or if they just guess something that makes sense, ignoring the letter sounds.

For *entertainment,* the chunks only helped with the pronunciation of the word. Sometimes, the word has morphemes—prefixes, suffixes, or root words—which also help with the meaning of the word. The next example shows what a teacher might do and say to introduce the word *international.*

Write on the board or overhead transparency: *The thinning of the ozone layer is an international problem.*

"Today, we are going to look at a big word that is really just a little word with a prefix added to the beginning and a suffix added to the end."

Underline *nation.*

"Who can tell me this word? Yes, that's the word *nation,* and we know *nation* is another word for *country.* Now let's look at the prefix that comes before *nation.*"

Underline *inter.*

"This prefix is *inter.* You probably know *inter* from words like *interrupt* and *internal.* Now let's look at what follows *inter* and *nation.*"

Underline *al.*

"You know *al* from many words, such as *unusual* and *critical.*"

Write *unusual* and *critical* and underline the *al.*

"Listen as I pronounce this part of the word."

Underline and pronounce *national.*

"Notice how the pronunciation of *nation* changes when we put *a-l* on it. Now let's put all the parts together and pronounce the word *inter nation al*." Let's read the sentence and make sure *international* makes sense."

Have the sentence read and confirm that ozone thinning is indeed a problem for many nations to solve.

"You can figure out the pronunciation of many big words if you look for common prefixes, such as *inter,* common root words, such as *nation,* and common suffixes, such as *al.*

"In addition to helping you figure out the pronunciation of a word, prefixes and suffixes sometimes help you know what the word means or where in a sentence we can use the word. The word *nation* names a thing. When we describe a nation, we add the suffix *al* and have *national.* The prefix *inter* often means "between or among." Something that is *international* is between many nations. The Olympics are the best example of an *international* sports event."

This sample lesson for introducing the word *international* demonstrates how a teacher can help students see and use morphemes to decode poly-syllabic words. As in the sample lesson for *entertainment,* the teacher points out words students might know that have the same chunks—in this case, morphemes. In addition, meaning clues yielded by the morphemes are provided whenever appropriate.

WORD DETECTIVES

There are two questions I would like to put into the mouths of every teacher of children from fourth grade through high school. These two questions are:

"Do I know any other words that look and sound like this word?"
"Are any of these look-alike/sound-alike words related to each other?"

The answer to the first question should help students with pronouncing and spelling the word. The answer to the second question should help students discover what, if any, meaning relationships exist between this new word and others in their meaning vocabulary stores. This guideline and these two simple questions could be used by any teacher of any subject area. Imagine that students in a mathematics class encounter the new word:

equation

The teacher demonstrates and gives examples of equations and helps build meaning for the concept. Finally, the teacher asks the students to pronounce equation and see if they know any other words that look and sound like equation. Students think of:

addition   multiplication   nation   vacation
equal   equator

The teacher lists the words, underlining the parts that look the same. Students pronounce the words, emphasizing the part that is pronounced the same. The teacher then points out to the students that thinking of a word that looks and sounds the same as a new word will help you quickly remember how to pronounce the new word and will also help you spell the new word.

Next the teacher explains that words, like people, sometimes look and sound alike but are not related. If this is the first time this analogy is used, the teacher will want to spend some time talking with the students about people with red hair, green eyes, and so on who have some parts that look alike but are not related and others who are.

"Not all people who look alike are related, but some are. This is how words work too. Words are related if there is something about their meaning that is the same. After we find look-alike, sound-alike words that will help us spell and pronounce new words, we try to think of any ways these words might be in the same meaning family."

With help from the teacher, the children discover that *equal, equator,* and *equation* are related because the meaning of *equal* is in all three. An equation has to have equal quantities on both sides of the equal signs. The equator is an imaginary line that divides the earth into two equal halves.

Imagine that the students who were introduced to equations on Monday during math and were asked to think of look-alike, sound-alike words and consider if any of these words might be "kinfolks" had a science lesson on Tuesday in which they did some experiments with the students using *thermometers* and *barometers.* At the close of the lesson, the teacher pointed to these words and helped them notice that the *meters* chunk was pronounced and spelled the same and asked the students if they thought these words were just look-alikes or were related to one another. The students would probably conclude that you used them both to measure things and the *meters* chunk must be related to measuring, like in *kilometers.* When asked to think of look-alike, sound-alike words for the first chunk, students thought of *baron* for *barometers* but decided these two words were probably not related. For *thermometer,* they thought of *thermal* and *thermostat* and decided that all these words had to do with heat or temperature and were related.

Now imagine that this lucky class of students had a social studies lesson on Wednesday during which the teacher pointed out the new word *international* and asked the two critical questions, a music lesson on Thursday in which they were preparing for a trip to the *symphony*, and a tennis lesson on Friday in which they practiced their *forehand* and *backhand* strokes and the teacher asked the two critical questions about these crucial tennis words.

Throughout their school day, children encounter many new words. Because English is such a morphologically related language, most new words can be connected to other words by their spelling and pronunciation, and many new words have meaning-related words already known to the student. Some clever, word-sensitive children become word detectives on their own. They notice the patterns and use these to learn and retrieve words. Others, however, try to learn to pronounce, spell, and associate meaning with each of these words as separate, distinct entities. This is a difficult task that becomes almost impossible as students move through the grades and the number of new words increases each year. Readers do not need to be taught every possible pattern because the brain is programmed to look for patterns. Some students, however, do not know what the important patterns in words are and that these patterns can help you with pronouncing, spelling, and meanings for words. Asking the two critical questions for key vocabulary introduced in any content area would add only a few minutes to the introduction of key content vocabulary and would turn many students into word detectives.

THE WHEEL

The popular game show *Wheel of Fortune* is premised on the idea that meaning and some letters allow you to figure out many words. In this game, meaning is provided by the category to which the words belong. A variation of this game can be used to introduce polysyllabic words and teach students to use meaning and all the letters they know. Here is how to play The Wheel.

Remind students that many words can be figured out, even when we can't decode all the chunks, if we think about what makes sense and whether it has the parts we do know in the right places. Ask students who have watched *Wheel of Fortune* to explain how it is played. Then explain, step by step, how your version of The Wheel will be different:

1. Contestants guess all letters without considering if they are consonants or vowels.
2. They must have all letters filled in before they can say the word. (This is to encourage them to learn to spell.)

3. They will win paper clips instead of great prizes.

4. Vanna will not be there to turn letters!

Write the category for the game on the board and draw blanks for each letter in the first word.

Have a student begin by asking,

"Is there a . . . ?"

If the student guesses a correct letter, fill that letter in. Give that student one paper clip for each time that letter occurs. Let the student continue to guess letters until he or she gets a "No." When a student asks for a letter that is not there, write the letter above the puzzle and go on to the next student.

Make sure that all letters are filled in before anyone is allowed to guess. (This really shows them the importance of spelling and attending to common spelling patterns.) Give the person who correctly guesses the word five bonus paper clips. Just as in other games, if someone says the answer out of turn, immediately award the bonus paper clips to the person whose turn it was. The student having the most paper clips at the end is the winner. Here is an example:

Teacher draws nine blanks on the board and says, "The category is sports. Our first word has nine letters. Al, guess a letter."

_ _ _ _ _ _ _ _ _

Al asks for a *t*. There is no *t*, so the teacher moves on to David who asks for an *r*. There is no *r* either. Nor is there an *o*, which Carol asks for. But Jon asks for and gets an *a*.

_ _ _ _ _ _ _ a _

Jon goes again and asks for an *s*.

s _ _ _ _ _ _ a _

Next, he asks for an *e*.

s e _ _ _ _ _ a _

Next, he asks for a *d*. There is no *d*, so the turn passes to Paula, who asks for an *n*.

s e _ _ _ _ n a _

Next, Paula asks for an *m*.

s e m _ _ _ n a _

Then she asks for an *i*.

s e m i _ i n a _

The light dawns in Paula's eyes. She quickly asks for an *f* and *l* and wins by correctly spelling and pronouncing *semifinal*!

TEACHING COMMON PREFIXES AND SUFFIXES

Four prefixes, *un*, *re*, *in* (and *im*, *ir*, *il* meaning "not"), and *dis* account for 58 percent of all prefixed words. Add 16 more prefixes—*en/em*, *non*, *in/im* (meaning "in"), *over*, *mis*, *sub*, *pre*, *inter*, *fore*, *de*, *trans*, *super*, *semi*, *anti*, *mid*, and *under*—and you can account for 97 percent of all prefixed words (White, Sowell, & Yanagihara,1989). Children who can read, spell, and attach meaning to these 20 prefixes have a jumpstart on decoding, spelling, and meaning for a huge number of multisyllabic words.

For suffixes, *s/es*, *ed*, and *ing* account for 65 percent of the suffixed words. Add *ly*, *er/or*, *ion/tion*, *ible/able*, *al*, *y*, *ness*, *ity*, and *ment* and you account for 87 percent of the words. The remaining suffixes with some utility are *er/est* (comparative), *ic*, *ous*, *en*, *ive*, *ful*, and *less* (White, Sowell, & Yanagihara,1989). Again, learning to read, spell, and understand how meaning is affected for a relatively small number of suffixes gives readers a huge advantage with multisyllabic words.

A Prefix Lesson Framework

The modeling during vocabulary introduction and Word Detectives activities described previously take advantage of whatever words occur in the course of content-area instruction. Most students can also profit from some explicit instruction with the most common prefixes. We teach all the prefixes using the same structure. We begin with words containing the prefixes students already can read and spell and have meaning for. We use these known words to establish the pattern and then move to less familiar words. We include examples of words in which the prefix has a discernible meaning and others in which the prefix helps with pronunciation and spelling but not with meaning. Here is an example lesson that could be used to sensitize students to the prefix *re*.

Write nine words that begin with *re* on index cards. Include three words in which *re* means "back," three words in which *re* means "again," and three words in which *re* is just the first syllable and has no apparent meaning. Use words for which your students are apt to have meanings:

rebound	redo	record
return	replay	refuse
replace	rework	reveal

Place these words randomly along the chalk ledge, have them pronounced, and ask students what "chunk" the words all have in common. Once students notice that they all begin with *r-e*, arrange the words in three columns on the board and tell the students to think about why you have put together *rebound*, *return*, and *replace* in one column, *redo*, *replay*, and *rework* in the second column, and *record*, *refuse*, and *reveal* in the third column. If students need help, tell them that for one column of *re* words, you can put the word *again* in place of the *re* and still have the meaning of the word. Explain that for another column, you can put the word *back* in place of *re*. Once students have figured out in which column the *re* means "back" and in which *re* means "again," label these columns *back* and *again*. Help students see that when you refuse something, you don't fuse it back or fuse it again. Do the same with *record* and *reveal*.

Have students set up their own papers in three columns, the first two headed by *back* and *again* and the last not headed, and have them write the words written on the board. Then say some other *re* words and have students write them in the column they think they belong in. As each word is written, ask someone where they wrote it and how they spelled it. Write it in the appropriate column on the board. Conclude the activity by having all the *re* words read and replacing the *re* with *back* or *again* when appropriate. Help students summarize that sometimes *re* means "back," sometimes *re* means "again," and sometimes *re* is just the first chunk of the word. Some additional words you might use are:

reusable	retire	retreat	rewind
recall	respond	remote	responsible
recoil	rewrite	refund	relief

Once this activity is completed, leave the chart with these *re* words displayed and ask students to hunt for *re* words in their reading for the next several days. When they find a word that begins with *re*, they should decide which category it fits and add it to the chart. At the end of several days, review the chart and help students summarize what they learned about *re* as a pronunciation, spelling, and sometimes meaning chunk in words.

As you do other lessons with prefixes, your message to students should be the same. Prefixes are chunks at the front of words that have predictable pronunciations and spellings. Look for them and depend on them to help you spell and pronounce new words. Sometimes, they also give you meaning clues. If you are unsure about the meaning of a word, see if a common meaning for the prefix can help. Check the meaning you figure out to make sure it makes sense in the context in which you are reading. Here are the most common prefixes, their most common meanings, and examples of words in which the prefix is a meaning help along with examples of words in which the prefix is only a help for spelling and pronouncing the word.

Prefix	Meaning	Meaning Chunk	Spelling/ Pronunciation Chunk
re	back	replacement	refrigerator
re	again	rearrange	reward
un	opposite	unfriendly	uncle
in (im, ir, il)	opposite	independent	incident
		impossible	imagine
		irresponsible	irritate
		illegal	illustrate
in (im)	in	invasion	instant
		impression	immense
dis	opposite	dishonest	distress
non	opposite	nonliving	—
en	in	encourage	entire
mis	bad, wrong	misunderstand	miscellaneous
pre	before	prehistoric	present
inter	between	international	interesting
de	opposite/take away	deodorize	delight
sub	under	submarine	subsist
fore	before/in front of	forehead	—
trans	across	transportation	—
super	really big	supermarkets	superintendent
semi	half	semifinal	seminar
mid	middle	midnight	midget
over	too much	overpower	—
under	below	underweight	understand
anti	against	antifreeze	—

The "Unpeelable" Prefixes

In addition to the above prefixes, which can be understood by taking them off the root word and then combining the meanings, there are other common prefixes that do not leave recognizable words when they are "peeled off." The prefixes *con/com, ex, em,* and *per* do add meanings to words, but you have to have a rather advanced understanding of Latin and Greek roots to see the meaning relationships. It is probably best to just help students see how these are predictable spelling and pronunciation chunks rather than try to show students how to analyze these words for meaning clues. Here are some examples for these "unpeelable" prefixes:

Unpeelable Prefix	Examples
com/con	communities, competition, communism
	composer, computer, compassion
	continuous, construction, conclusion
	conversation, constitution, concrete
em	employee, embassy, embryo
ex	expensive, excitement, explain
per	performance, permanent, personality

A Suffix Lesson Framework

Suffixes, like prefixes, are predictable indicators of pronunciation and sometimes signal a meaning relationship. The meaning signaled by suffixes, however, is not usually a meaning change, but rather a change in how and in what position the word can be used in the sentence. *Compose* is what you do. The *composer* is the person doing it. A *composition* is what you have once you have composed. Students need to become aware of how words change when they are signaling different relationships. They also need to realize that there are slight pronunciation changes in root words when suffixes are added.

The first suffixes we teach should be the most familiar to students and have the highest utility. The suffixes *er* and *ion* make particularly useful first lessons.

To teach *er*, write words on index cards that demonstrate the someone or something who does something, some comparative meanings, and some words that just end in *er*. Place the words randomly along the chalk ledge and have students notice that the words all end in *er*. Next, arrange the words in four columns, and help students see that column-one words are all people who do something, column-two words are things that do something, column-three words mean "more," and column-four words are those in which *er* is just the last chunk:

reporter	computer	fatter	cover
photographer	pointer	skinnier	never
teacher	heater	greater	master

Label the first three columns *People Who Do, Things That Do,* and *More.* Do not label the last column. Have pupils set up papers in four columns, labeling and listing the words just as you have done on the board. Call out some *er* words and have students write them in the column they think they belong in. Then have students spell each word and tell you which column to put the word in. Remind students of spelling rules—changing *y* to *i*, doubling letters—as needed. Some *er* words you might use are:

after	richer	fighter	winner
winter	under	heavier	air conditioner
murderer	manager	copier	dish washer
runner	diaper	writer	typewriter

A common suffix that is always pronounced the same way and that sometimes signals a change from doing to the thing done is *ion*. Students make this shift easily in their speech and need to recognize that the same shift occurs in reading and writing. Write *tion* words on index cards, some of which have a related "doing" word and some of which don't. After students notice that the words all end in *tion* and that the *tion* chunk is pronounced the same, divide the words to form two columns on the board. For example:

collection	nation
election	fraction
attraction	vacation

Help students see that when you collect coins, you have a coin *collection;* we elect leaders during an *election;* and you have an *attraction* for someone you are attracted to. In *nation, fraction,* and *vacation,* the *tion* is pronounced the same but the meaning of the word is not obvious by looking at the root word. Have students set up their papers in the usual way, then call out words for students to decide which group they fit with. Be sure to have students spell words as you write them on the board and talk about the meaning relationships where appropriate. Here are some starters:

traction	subtraction	construction	rejection
auction	expedition	tradition	interruption
mention	action	pollution	correction

Here are some *sion* words you could use in a similar activity:

confusion	invasion	vision	provision
extension	suspension	passion	expression
collision	mission	tension	explosion

Just as with prefixes, we keep the chart displayed for several days and ask students to add words they find in their reading to the appropriate columns. Here are the most common endings and suffixes, along with example words whose meaning is familiar to most children.

Suffix/Ending	Examples
s/es	heroes, musicians, signatures
(y-i)	communities, discoveries, countries
ed/ing	unfinished, performed, misunderstanding
(drop e)	nonliving, replaced, continuing
(double consonant)	swimming, forgetting,
er/est	richest, craziest, bigger
en	forgotten, hidden, chosen
less	hopeless, careless, penniless
ful	beautiful, successful, pitiful
able	valuable, portable, incurable
ible	irresponsible, reversible, horrible
tion	transportation, imagination, solution
sion	invasion, impression, permission
ly	unfriendly, hopelessly, happily
er	composer, reporter, robber
or	governor, dictator, juror
ee	employee, referee, trainee
ian	musician, magician, beautician
ance	performance, attendance, ignorance
ence	independence, conference, persistence
ment	encouragement, punishment, involvement
ness	happiness, goodness, business
y	discovery, jealousy, pregnancy
ity	electricity, popularity, possibility
ant	unpleasant, tolerant, dominant
ent	different, confident, excellent
al	international, political, racial
ive	expensive, inconclusive, competitive
ous	continuous, humorous, ambitious
ic	prehistoric, scenic, specific
ify	classify, beautify, identify
ize	deodorize, modernize, standardize
ture	signature, creature, fracture

TEACHING COMMON ROOT WORDS

So far, we have talked about working from prefixes and suffixes back to the root word. Some children find it exciting to see how many different words they can read and understand from just one root word. Students need to learn that the pronunciation of a root word often changes slightly as prefixes and suffixes are added. They also need to learn that the root sometimes helps them to come up with meanings. Some sample root-word activities are described next.

Lessons With Simple Roots

For the first lessons, use some words that students know well to make the point that words they know are often the keys to unlocking the pronunciation, spelling, and meaning for hundreds of other words. *Play* makes a great first lesson.

Write the word *play* on the board. Tell students that a little word like *play* can become a big word when parts are added to the beginning and ending of the word. Write words that have *play* in them. Have the words pronounced and talk about how the meaning of the word changes. Have students suggest other words with *play*. Here are some starters:

plays	played	playing	player	players
playful	playfully	playable	replay	playfulness
misplay	ballplayer	outplay	overplay	playground
playhouse	playoff	playpen	playwright	screenplay

Other roots that have many words include *work*, *agree*, and *create*:

workable	homework	network	rework
working	legwork	housework	outwork
workers	unworkable	nonworker	woodwork
teamwork	overworked	paperwork	schoolwork
workshop	workout	groundwork	hardworking
agree	agreeable	agreeably	disagreement
agreed	agreement	nonagreement	agreeableness
agreeing	disagreeable	disagreeably	disagreeableness
creatures	creates	created	recreation
creator	creative	creating	creatively
creativity	uncreative	creation	recreational

Lessons With More Complex Roots

Sometimes there are root words whose meaning must be taught so that students can see how words in that family are related in meaning. The most useful of these is the root word *port*.

Write the words *reporter*, *portable*, and *export* on the board. Pronounce the words as you underline *port* in each. Tell students that many words in English have the word *port* in them. Tell them to listen as you tell them some meaning for the three words on the board to see if they can hear a meaning all the words share.

A reporter carries a story back to tell others.
Something you can carry with you is portable.
When you export something, you take or carry it out of the country.

Help students to understand that *port* often means "carry or take." Next write this list of words on the board one at a time and help students to see how the meanings change but are still related to *port*:

port	import
export	importer
exportable	transport
nonexportable	transportation

Label this list of words *Carry/Take*.

Begin another list with the words *portion* and *portrait*. Underline *port*. Help students to see that not all words which have *port* in them have a meaning clearly related to *carry* or *take*. Tell students that when they see a word containing *port* whose meaning they do not know, they should try to figure out a meaning related to *take* or *carry* and see if that meaning makes sense in the sentence. Have students set up their paper in two columns like your board. Then call out some words, some of which have the meaning of carry or take and some of which don't. Here are some possibilities:

importer	exporter	airport	deport
unimportant	porter	portray	passport
misreport	support	nonsupport	opportunity
seaport	important	portfolio	Portugal

You could do a similar activity with the root *press*. Write the words *depression*, *impress*, and *repress* on the board. Pronounce the words as you underline *press* in each. Tell students that many words in English have the word *press* in them. Tell them to listen as you tell them some meanings for the words on the board to see if they can hear a meaning all the words share.

"You make a depression when you push something down. You feel depression when you feel pushed down. When you repress a feeling, you push it out of your mind. You impress people when you push your good image into their minds."

Help students to understand that *press* often means "push." Next write these words on the board and help students to see how the meanings change but are still related to press:

press	oppress
express	oppressive
expressible	oppressiveness
inexpressible	

Tell students that when they see a word containing *press* whose meaning they do not know, they should try to figure out a meaning related to push and see if that meaning makes sense in the sentence they are reading.

Begin another column with the word *cypress*. Have students notice that *cypress* ends in *press* but there does not appear to be any "push" meaning in *cypress*. Here are some words, only one of which does not have any "push" meaning relationship.

expression	expressway	inexpressible	antidepressant
compression	pressure	pressurize	suppress
impressive	unimpressed	repressive	empress

Some other root words that are easy for students to understand and that have many related words are:

act: action, react, activity, active, inactive, activate
sign: signature, design, resign, designate, signal, insignia, significant
form: reform, inform, information, deform, uniform, formula, transform
meter: barometer, thermometer, kilometer, centimeter, millimeter, diameter

THE NIFTY THRIFTY FIFTY

All the activities described in this chapter so far will help children develop a store of big words they can read and spell, and teach them how to analyze big words for familiar patterns. Because a limited number of prefixes, suffixes, and spelling changes can be found in thousands of multisyllabic words, all children should have example words for these that are thoroughly familiar to them. What words could older children learn to read, spell, and analyze so that we could be sure they had examples for these common patterns?

I created such a list by deciding which prefixes, suffixes, and spelling changes were most prevalent in the multisyllabic words students might encounter. I included all the prefixes and suffixes determined to be most common in the White, Sowell, and Yanagihara study. Because I wanted to create a list that would provide the maximum help with all three big-word tasks, I added prefixes and suffixes such as *con/com, per, ex, ture, ian* not included in that study because they were not considered helpful from a meaning standpoint. These prefixes are useful spelling and pronunciation chunks.

Having created the list of "transferable chunks," I then wanted to find the "most-apt-to-be-known" word containing each chunk. I consulted *The Living Word Vocabulary* (Dale & O'Rourke, 1981), which indicates for 44,000 words the grade level at which more than two-thirds of the students tested knew the meaning of the word. Because the test from which it was determined students knew the meanings also required them to read the word, it can also be inferred that at least two-thirds of the students could decode and pronounce the word. The goal was to find words that two-thirds of fourth graders could read and knew at least one meaning for. After much finagling, a list of 50 words was created that contains all the most useful prefixes, suffixes, and spelling changes. All but eight of these words were known by more than two-thirds of fourth graders. Seven words—*antifreeze, classify, deodorize, impression, irresponsible, prehistoric,* and *semifinal*—were not known by two-thirds of fourth graders but were known by two-thirds of sixth graders. *International,* the most known word containing the prefix *inter,* was known by two-thirds of eighth graders. Because this list of 50 words is apt to be known by so many intermediate-age and older students, and because it so economically represents all the important big-word parts, I named this list the Nifty Thrifty Fifty.

The Nifty Thrifty Fifty

Word	Prefix	Suffix or ending
antifreeze	anti	
beautiful		ful (y-i)
classify		ify
communities	com	es (y-i)
community	com	
composer	com	er
continuous	con	ous
conversation	con	tion
deodorize	de	ize
different		ent
discovery	dis	y
dishonest	dis	
electricity		ity
employee	em	ee
encouragement	en	ment
expensive	ex	ive
forecast	fore	
forgotten		en (double t)
governor		or
happiness		ness (y-i)
hopeless		less
illegal	il	
impossible	im	
impression	im	sion
independence	in	ence
international	inter	al
invasion	in	sion
irresponsible	ir	ible

midnight	mid	
misunderstand	mis	
musician		ian
nonliving	non	ing (drop e)
overpower	over	
performance	per	ance
prehistoric	pre	ic
prettier		er (y-i)
rearrange	re	
replacement	re	ment
richest		est
semifinal	semi	
signature		ture
submarine	sub	
supermarkets	super	s
swimming		ing (double m)
transportation	trans	tion
underweight	under	
unfinished	un	ed
unfriendly	un	ly
unpleasant	un	ant
valuable		able (drop e)

There are endless possibilities for how the list might be used. First, however, students must learn to spell the words. Teachers might want to start a word wall (see Chapter 2) of big words and add five words each week to the wall. They might take a few minutes each day to chant the spelling of the words and talk about the parts of the word that could be applied to other words. This talking should be as nonjargony as possible. Rather than talking about the root word *freeze* and the prefix *anti*, the discussions should be about how antifreeze keeps your car's engine from freezing up and thus it is protection against freezing. Students should be asked to think of other words that look and sound like *antifreeze* and then decide if the *anti* parts of those words could have anything to do with the notion of "against."

"What is an antibiotic against?" "What is an antiaircraft weapon?"

For suffixes, the discussion should center around how the suffix changes how the word can be used in a sentence.

"A *musician* makes music. What does a beautician, electrician, physician, or magician do?"

"When you need to replace something, you get a replacement. What do you get when someone encourages you?" "What do you call it when you accomplish something?"

Spelling changes should be noticed and applied to similar words.

"*Communities* is the plural of *community*. How would you spell *parties*? *Candies*? *Personalities*?"

"When we forget something, we say it was forgotten. How would you spell *bitten*? *Written*?"

If this list is to become truly useful to students, they need to learn to spell the words gradually over time, and they need to be shown how the patterns found in these words can be useful in decoding, spelling, and figuring out meaning for lots of other words. Here is an example of how the first words might be taught:

1. Explain that in English, many big words are just smaller words with prefixes and suffixes. The Nifty Thrifty Fifty words include all the important prefixes and suffixes and spelling changes needed to read, spell, and figure out meanings for thousands of other words.

2. Add 5–6 words to your display each week. Use different colors and make the words big and bold so that they are easily seen.

3. Have students chant each word cheerleader style with you. After cheering for each word, help students analyze the word, talking about meaning and determining the root, prefix, and suffix, and noting any spelling changes.

   composer—A composer is a person who composes something. Many other words such as *writer*, *reporter*, and *teacher* are made up of a root word and the suffix *er*, meaning a person or thing that does something.

expensive—The word *expense* with the suffix *ive* added and the *e* in *expense* dropped. Another related word that students might not know is *expend*. You might be able to make the *expend-expense-expensive* relationship clear to them by using the sports terms *defend, defense, defensive*.

encouragement—When you encourage someone, you give them encouragement. Many other words such as *argue, argument*; *replace, replacement* follow this same pattern. The root word for *encourage* is *courage*. So *encouragement* is made up of the prefix *en*, the root word *courage*, and the suffix *ment*.

impossible—The root *possible* with the suffix *im*. In many words, including *impatient* and *immature*, the suffix *im* changes the word to an opposite.

musician—A musician is a person who makes music. A beautician helps make you beautiful and a magician makes magic. *Musician* has the root word *music* with the suffix *ian*, which sometimes indicates the person who does something. There are no spelling changes, but the pronunciation changes. Have students say the words *music* and *musician*, *magic*, and *magician* and notice how the pronunciation changes.

4. Once you have noticed the composition for each word, helped students see other words that work in a similar way, and cheered for each word, have students write each word. Students enjoy writing the words more and focus better on the word if you give clues to the word such as:

   Number 1 is the opposite of discouragement

   For number 2, write the word that tells what you are if you play the guitar.

   For number 3, write what you are if you play the guitar but you also make up the songs you play.

   Write the word that is the opposite of possible for number 4.

   The last word means costing a lot of money.

5. After writing all the words, have students check their own papers by once more chanting the letters aloud, underlining each as they say it.

When you have a few minute of "sponge" time, practice the words by chanting or writing. As you are cheering or writing each word, ask students to identify the root, prefix, and suffix and talk about how these affect the meaning of the root word. Point out any spelling changes.

The following week, add another five or six words and follow the procedures above. When you have enough words, begin to show students how parts from the Nifty Thrifty Fifty words can be combined to spell lots of other words. From just the 11 words *composer, discovery, encouragement, expensive, hopeless, impossible, impression, musician, richest, transportation,* and *unfriendly,* students should be able to decode, spell, and discuss meanings for:

compose	pose	discover	encourage	courage
import	importation	possible	compress	compression
friendly	transpose	dispose	discourage	discouragement
enrich	enrichment	uncover	richly	hopelessly
impress	inexpensive	transport	port	expose
express	expression	export	exportation	

As more and more words are added, students become quite impressed with the number of transfer words they can read spell and build meanings

---

Nifty Thrifty Fifty Transfer Words

Here are just some of the words buildable from just the parts of the fifty words. The number grows astronomically when the prefixes and suffixes are attached to other root words students know.

conform	conformity	inform	informer	informant
information	misinform	uninformed	formation	formal
transformation	transform	performer	responsibility	responsive
responsiveness	honesty	dishonesty	honestly	legally
illegally	responsibly	irresponsibly	arranging	rearranging
placing	replacing	misplacing	report	reporter
refinish	relive	refreeze	reclassify	revalue
recover	rediscover	electrical	displease	discontinue
disposal	musical	continual	employer	employment
unemployment	unemployed	employable	difference	unemployable
consignment	nationality	nationalities	internationalize	nationalize
interdependence	depress	depression	deodorant	deport
deportation	deportee	devalue	declassify	decompose
deform	deformity	prearrange	resign	resignation
designation	significant	significance	freezer	freezing

freezable	subfreezing	underclass	overexpose	underexpose
superimpose	undercover	forecaster	forecasting	forecastable
empowerment	miscast	overture	empower	antidepressant
powerful	powerfully	powerfulness	powerless	powerlessly
powerlessness	superpower	finalize	finalizing	finalization
weighty	weightless	beautician	electrician	undervalue
unfriendliness	friendlier	friendliest	friendliness	unpleasantness
historical	historically	expressive	impressive	repressive
invasive	noninvasive	invasiveness	hopefully	hopelessly

for. (For more Nifty Thrifty Fifty lessons, see *Phonics For Upper Grades* by Cunningham & Hall, 1998.)

Facility with big words is essential for students as they read, write, and learn in all areas of school and life. Many big words occur infrequently, but when they do occur, they carry a lot of the meaning and content of what is being read. English is a language in which many words are related through their morphology. Linguists estimate that every big word a child can read, spell, and analyze enables the reader to acquire six or seven other morphemically related words. Students who learn to look for patterns in the big new words they meet will be better spellers and decoders. If they learn to look further and consider possible meaning relationships, they will increase the size of their meaning vocabulary stores.

REFERENCES

Canney, G., & Schreiner, R. (1977). A study of the effectiveness of selected syllabication rules and phonogram patterns for word attack. *Reading Research Quarterly, 12,* 102–124.

Cunningham. P. M., & Hall, D. P. (1998). *Month by Month Phonics for Upper Grades: A Second Chance for Struggling Readers and Students Learning English.* Greensboro, NC: Carson-Dellosa.

Dale, E., & O'Rourke, J. (1981) *The living word vocabulary.* Chicago: Worldbook.

Nagy, W., & Anderson, R. C. (1984). How many words are there in printed school English? *Reading Research Quarterly, 19,* 304–330.

Shepard, J. F. (1974). Research on the relationship between meanings of morphemes and the meaning of derivatives. In P. L. Nacke (Ed.), *23d N.R.C. Yearbook* (pp. 115–119). Clemson, SC: National Reading Conference.

White, T., Sowell, J., & Yanagihara, A. (1989) Teaching elementary students to use word-part clues. *The Reading Teacher, 42,* 302–308.

THE THEORY AND THE RESEARCH— THE WHY UNDERLYING THE HOW

> The question of instruction in phonics has aroused a lot of controversy. Some educators have held to the proposition that phonetic training is not only futile and wasteful but also harmful to the best interests of a reading program. Others believe that since the child must have some means of attacking strange words, instruction in phonics is imperative. There have been disputes also relative to the amount of phonics to be taught, the time when the teaching should take place and the methods to be used. In fact, the writer knows of no problem around which more disputes have centered.
>
> *Paul McKee—1934 (p. 191)*

Clearly, the phonics question has been plaguing the field of reading for a long time. In this chapter, I will share with you my own history as a student, a teacher, and a researcher with the phonics dilemma, review the major research findings of the past 30 years, and explain the relationship between the research and the type of phonics instruction found in this book.

MY PERSONAL PHONICS HISTORY

My fate was probably sealed in 1949 when I was a first grader at High Street School in Westerly, Rhode Island. In the morning, we were divided into reading groups and read about the adventures of Sally, Dick, Jane, Puff, and Spot. After lunch each day, we all pulled out bright-blue phonics books and sounded out words. Little did I know that at five years old, I was thrust right into the middle of the sight word–phonics controversy.

The year 1965 found me teaching first grade in Key West, Florida. I taught the phonics in my basal manual, and most children learned to distinguish short vowels from long vowels. The children in my top group even developed the ability to sound out new words, although even then I didn't quite believe that what they did when they came to a new word was in any way related to what I was teaching them about phonics. One day, I overheard a boy remark to a friend,

> "The short vowels are pretty short, but the long ones look pretty short, too."

His friend then proceeded to explain it to him.

> "It's simple. The little ones are the short ones and the capital ones are the long ones."

Although I continued to teach first grade and the vowel rules for several years, my faith in them was badly shaken!

I got my master's degree in Reading from Florida State in 1968. "Linguistics" was the buzzword at that time, and I thought that "linguistic readers" were going to solve the decoding problems of our poor readers. I got a chance to try this out with a whole class full of fourth-grade poor readers. Armed with the Merrill Linguistic Readers and the SRA Basic Reading Series, I abandoned phonics rules for linguistic patterns. Things went pretty well for the first month. The students learned all the short *a* patterns and read about Dan in his tan van. As we moved on, however, they began to confuse the previously learned patterns with the new ones. Worse yet, I realized that the children had stopped trying to make sense of what they were reading and were simply sounding out the patterns.

By 1970, context was the only remaining tool in my decoding arsenal. "Say 'blank' and read the rest of the sentence and then go back and think about what would make sense," was my 1970 brand of decoding instruction. In 1971, I found myself in Terre Haute, Indiana, as the special reading teacher at the Indiana State University Laboratory School. All day, I worked with poor readers. Mostly, I tried to get these students to enjoy reading and to talk about what they read. I did almost no phonics instruction, but it did worry me that almost all the poor readers had little ability to decode an unfamiliar word.

My "real challenges" arrived after lunch each day. Rod and Erin were sixth graders of normal intelligence who had been in remedial reading since second grade and who read at the second-grade level. Both boys were fluent with all the most commonly occurring words and were excellent users of picture and context clues. They could understand anything they could read and most of what you read to them. They had been scheduled for 45 minutes alone with me each day because they were to go on to junior high next year and their parents were very worried that, after all these years, they still hadn't "caught on to reading."

For both Rod and Erin, the problem was clear-cut. They knew what reading was and that you were to make meaning from it. They enjoyed being read to and even enjoyed reading the high-interest, low-vocabulary books I could find that they could read themselves. They simply had not learned to decode! For the first semester, I taught Rod and Erin "word families." They were very competitive and I made Go Fish and Old Maid and Concentration games, which they could win by matching and saying rhyming words. We also made charts of rhyming words and wrote jingles and riddles, which were awful but which appealed to their sixth-grade silliness.

In addition to rhyming games and writing rhymes, each day we read together and I reminded them of the one strategy I had taught them. Both boys knew that when you came to a short word you didn't know, you should look to see if it would rhyme with a word you did know. When they couldn't think of a rhyming word, I prompted them with one. They used this strategy when they were reading and were amazed to discover that they could figure out even unusual names—*Tran, Clark, Kurt.*

Unfortunately, their newfound decoding ability did not transfer to bigger words. I taught them a few simple syllable-division rules, and they could sometimes figure out a two-syllable word, the syllables of which were familiar rhyming patterns—*zinger, target, pastor.* If a word had more than six letters, however, they couldn't even begin to do anything with it and would just skip it and go on.

By March, the boys were reading at a strong third-grade level—sometimes fourth—if they knew a lot about the topic. I knew that their inability and unwillingness to decode long words was the remaining hurdle, but I didn't know how to teach them to figure them out. I taught them some prefixes and suffixes, but this didn't seem to help with very many words. Driving home in the afternoons, I would see a big word on a billboard and ask myself, "How did I figure out that word?" I knew that I had not applied syllabication rules and then sounded out each syllable, but I didn't know what I had done.

We were at six weeks before the end of sixth grade, and Rod and Erin had begun the countdown to summer and junior high! In desperation, I searched the Education Index for "polysyllabic word instruction." I didn't find much, and discounted most of what I did find. Context was what Rod and Erin were currently using. Syllabication rules weren't working (and research confirmed that). They had learned many of the common prefixes and suffixes, but they didn't seem to use them. Finally, one article suggested teaching students to use the dictionary respelling key. "Well, that's something I haven't tried," I thought. "But no one is ever going to stop reading and find the word in the dictionary and use the respelling key," I argued with myself.

But I decided to do it. What did I have to lose? We had to do something useful for the last six weeks, and at least they would know how to use the respelling key to pronounce a word if they would take the time to do it. For two weeks, I taught them how to use the key to figure out the pronunciation of unknown words. Then, when they understood how to do it, I gave them each a different list of five "really long" words (*conscientious*, *filibuster*, *mannequin*, *Phoenician*, *sporadically*) each day. Before we could go on to do anything interesting, they each had to find their words and use the key to figure them out and pronounce them for me.

They hated it but "it was good for them," and I was determined that they would have a big-word tool to take with them to junior high, so each day, they came in and picked up their list and their dictionaries and went to work. Ten days before the end of school, Rod walked in and picked up his list of five "humongous" words and his dictionary. He began to look up the first word, then he stopped, looked at the word, and then at me. "What if I already know this word? Do I still have to look it up?" he asked.

"Well no," I responded. "I'm trying to give you a tool so that you can always pronounce any big word you ever come to, but if you know the word, you don't need the respelling key, do you?" Rod looked again at the first word, studying the letters. He then correctly pronounced "spontaneous." "That's right!" I exclaimed. "Now, you only have four to look up!" "Not if I know some of the others," Rod asserted. He was able to pronounce two of the other four words and only had to look up and use the key for two of the five big words. Meanwhile, Erin was studying his five words and he managed to pronounce two of his, only having to look up three.

I was astonished! "Where had they learned those words?" I wondered. For the remaining nine days of school, Rod and Erin competed to see how many words they could figure out and not have to look up. To my amazement, by the last day of school they had gotten quite good at figuring out words of four or more syllables. The respelling key gave them a system for independently figuring out big words. At the time, I didn't understand how this miracle had occurred, but I sent Rod and Erin off to junior high more confident of their success than I had ever thought I would.

In 1972, I arrived at the University of Georgia to work on my doctorate in reading. When Dr. Ira Aaron led us to do some initial thinking about a dissertation topic, I already knew what I wanted to find out: "How do we decode an unknown word, and particularly an unknown big word?" After much reading, thinking, and discussions with other doctoral students and Dr. George Mason, my advisor, I became convinced that decoding took place in what I called a compare/contrast way. Later this would be called "decoding by analogy." In addition to my dissertation (Cunningham, 1975–76), I did quite a bit of research into analogic decoding (Cunningham, 1979; 1980; Cunningham & Guthrie, 1982; Gaskins et al., 1988), which confirmed for me that decoding was neither a letter-by-letter sounding process nor a rule-based, jargon-filled process. My observations of the children I had taught, as well as the research I carried out, convinced me that when readers come to unfamiliar words, they do a fast search through their cognitive word stores for similar words with the same letters in the same places. They then use these analogs to come up with a possible pronunciation that they try out and cross-check with meaning.

I understood finally that when I complained that my first graders knew the rules but didn't use them, I was right! The rules describe the system. The brain, however, is not a rule applier but a pattern detector. I also understood why teaching children linguistic patterns or "word families" was a powerful strategy if you could get them to use these spelling patterns to write and read words in meaningful texts.

By 1982, 10 years after Rod and Erin had learned to read, I had figured out how they did it. Combining word-family instruction with reading and writing in which they were encouraged to use rhyming words to figure out how to pronounce or spell unknown words taught them to look for patterns in words and, most importantly, that there were patterns to be found when they looked. Looking up big words in the dictionary respelling key forced them to look carefully at all the letters in the words (so that they could find them in the dictionary), and the analogs contained in the respelling key convinced them that there were patterns to be found in big words, too.

WHAT WE KNOW ABOUT HOW GOOD READERS READ WORDS

We know a great deal more about how word recognition occurs than can be explained in this section. The theory that explains the incredibly fast ability of the brain to recognize words and associate them with meaning is called parallel distributed processing. This theory is complex, but its most important tenets are easily understood. Information about a word is gained from its spelling (orthography), its pronunciation (phonology), its meaning (semantics), and the context in which the word occurs. The brain processes these sources of information in parallel, or simultaneously. The brain functions in word recognition, as it does in all other areas, as a pattern detector.

Discussion of parallel distributed processing and its implications for word identification can be found in Seidenberg and McClelland (1989), McClelland and Rumelhart (1986), and Rumelhart and McClelland (1986). The theory is translated and explained simply and elegantly in Adams (1990). Beyond the fact that the brain responds to many sources of information in parallel and that it functions as a pattern detector, the following specific facts seem particularly pertinent to the question of what kind of phonics instruction we should have.

Readers look at virtually all of the words and almost all the letters in those words   (Rayner & Pollatsek, 1989; McConkie, Kerr, Reddix, & Zola, 1987). For many years, it was generally believed that sophisticated readers sampled text. Based on predictions about what words and letters they would see, readers were thought to look at the words and letters just enough to see if their predictions were confirmed. Eye-movement research carried out with computerized tracking has proven that, in reality, readers look at every word and almost every letter of each word. The amount of time spent processing each letter is incredibly small, only a few hundredths of a second. The astonishingly fast letter recognition for letters within familiar words and patterns is explained by the fact that our brains expect certain letters to occur in sequence with other letters.

Readers usually recode printed words into sound   (Tannenhaus, Flanigan, & Seidenberg, 1980; McCutchen, Bell, France, & Perfetti, 1991). Although it is possible to read without any internal speech, we rarely do. Most of the time as we read, we think the words in our mind. This phonological information is then checked with the information we received visually by analyzing the word for familiar spelling patterns. Saying the words aloud or thinking the words also seems to perform an important function in holding the words in auditory memory until enough words are read to create meaning.

Readers recognize most words immediately and automatically without using context   (LaBerge & Samuels, 1974; Stanovich,1991; Samuels, 1988; Nicholson, 1991). Good readers use context to see if what they are reading makes sense. Context is also important for disambiguating the meaning of some words (I had a *ball* throwing the *ball* at the *ball*). Occasionally, readers use context to figure out what the word is. Most of the time, however, words are identified based on their familiar spelling and the association of that spelling with a pronunciation. Context comes into play after, not before, the word is identified based on the brain's processing of the letter-by-letter information it receives. Several studies have found that poor readers rely more on context than good readers.

Readers accurately and quickly pronounce infrequent, phonetically regular words   (Hogaboam & Perfetti, 1978; Daneman, 1991). When presented with unfamiliar but phonetically regular words, good readers immediately and seemingly effortlessly assign them a pronunciation. The ability to quickly and accurately pronounce phonetically regular words that are not sight words is a task that consistently discriminates among good and poor readers.

Readers use spelling patterns and analogy to decode words   (Adams, 1990; Goswami & Bryant, 1990; Moustafa, 1997). The answer to the question of whether phonics should be taught in a synthetic or analytic manner seems to be neither. Synthetic approaches generally teach children to go letter by letter, assigning a pronunciation to each letter and then blending the individual letters together. Analytic approaches teach rules and are usually filled with confusing jargon. (The *e* on the end makes the vowel long.) Brain research, however, suggests that the brain is a pattern detector, not a rule applier and that, while we look at single letters, we are looking at them considering all the letter patterns we know. Successfully decoding a word occurs when the brain recognizes a familiar spelling pattern or, if the pattern itself is not familiar, searches through its store of words with similar patterns.

To decode the unfamiliar word *knob*, for example, the child who knew many words that began with *kn* would immediately assign to the *kn* the "n" sound. The initial *kn* would be stored in the brain as a spelling pattern. If the child knew only a few other words with *kn* and hadn't read these words very often, that child would probably not have *kn* as a known spelling pattern and thus would have to do a quick search for known words which began with *kn*. If the child found the words *know* and *knew* and then tried this same sound on the unknown word *knob*, that child would have used the analogy strategy. Likewise, the child might know the pronunciation for *ob* because of having correctly read so many words containing the *ob* spelling pattern or might have had to access some words with *ob* to use them to come up with the pronunciation. The child who had no stored spelling patterns for *kn* or *ob* and no known words to access and compare to would be unlikely to successfully pronounce the unknown word *knob*.

Readers divide big words as they see them based on interletter frequencies (Mewhort & Campbell, 1981; Seidenberg, 1987). The research on syllabication rules shows that it is quite possible to know the rules and still be unable to quickly and accurately pronounce novel polysyllabic words, and equally possible to be able to pronounce them and not know the rules. Good readers "chunk" or divide words into manageable units. They do this based on the brain's incredible knowledge of which letters usually go together in words. If you did not recognize the word *midnight* in print, you would divide it as you saw it, between the *d* and the *n*. For the word *Madrid*, however, you would divide after the *a*, leaving the *dr* together. Interletter frequency theory explains this neatly by pointing out that the letters *dr* often occur together in syllables in words you know (*drop, dry, Dracula*). Words with the letters *dn* in the same syllable are almost nonexistent. This also explains why beginners might pronounce f-a-t-h-e-r as "fat her," but children who have some words from which the brain can generate interletter frequencies will leave the *th* together and pronounce "father."

To summarize what the brain does to identify words is to run the risk of oversimplification, but seems necessary before considering what we know about instruction. As we read, we look very quickly at almost all letters of each word. For most words, this visual information is recognized as a familiar pattern with which a spoken word is identified and pronounced. Words we have read before are instantly recognized as we see them. Words we have not read before are almost instantly pronounced based on spelling patterns the brain has seen in other words. If the word is a big word, the brain uses its interletter frequency knowledge (based on all the words it knows) to chunk the word into parts whose letter patterns can then be compared. Meaning is accessed through visual word recognition, but the sound of the word supports the visual information and helps to hold the word in memory.

WHAT WE KNOW ABOUT HOW CHILDREN LEARN TO READ WORDS

At present, we know more about how the word identification process works than we do about how children learn to do it. Here are some research-based findings that should have an impact on instruction.

Children from literate homes have over 1,000 hours of informal reading and writing encounters before coming to school   (Adams, 1990). We have always known that children who were read to came to school more ready, willing, and able to learn to read. In the past decade, however, findings from emergent literacy research have made it clear that the reading and writing encounters many children have include more than just a bedtime story. Estimates are that children from literate homes experience almost an hour each day of informal reading and writing encounters—being read to, trying to read a favorite book, watching someone write a thank-you letter, trying to write, manipulating magnetic letters, and talking with someone about environmental print such as grocery or restaurant labels, signs, and so forth. From these encounters, the children learn a tremendous amount of critical information. They know what reading and writing are really for and that you use words and letters. They know that you have to write these words and letters in a particular way, from top to bottom and left to right (though they often don't know this jargon). They also learn some words—important words like their name and the name of their pet dog and favorite fast-food restaurant. They learn the names of many of the letters of the alphabet and write these letters, usually in capital form. In addition to learning that words are made up of letters, which you can see, they somehow figure out that words are also made up of sounds, which you can't see.

Phonemic awareness is critical to success in beginning reading   (Bryant, Bradley, Maclean, & Crossland, 1989; Cunningham, Cunningham, Hoffman, & Yopp, 1998). One of the understandings that many children gain from early reading and writing encounters is the understanding that words are made up of sounds. These sounds are not separate and distinct. In fact, their existence is quite abstract. Phonemic awareness has many levels, and includes the ability to hear whether or not words rhyme, to know what word you would have if you removed a sound, and to manipulate phonemes to form different words. Phonemic awareness seems to be developed through lots of exposure to nursery rhymes and books that make words sound fun. Many of the "I can read" books (*Green Eggs and Ham; Inside, Outside, Upside Down; There's a Wocket in My Pocket; The Berenstain Bears B Book*, etc.) that come monthly to the homes of many preschoolers are made to order for helping children develop phonemic awareness. While children may be able to learn some letter sounds before they develop phonemic awareness, phonemic awareness must be present before children can manipulate those sounds as they try to read and write words.

Children who can decode well learn sight words better   (Jorm & Share, 1983; Stanovich & West, 1989; Ehri, 1991). Research indicates that the sight word versus phonics debate lacks reality when you consider how children learn words. When a new word is encountered for the first time, it is usually decoded. In decoding the word, the child forms phonological access routes for that word into memory. These access routes are built using knowledge of grapheme-phoneme correspondences that connect letters in spelling to phonemes in pronunciations of the words. The letters are processed as visual symbols for the phonemes, and the sequence of letters is retained in memory as an alphabetic, phonological representation of the word. When the child encounters that word again, the connection between letters and phonemes is strengthened. Eventually, the spelling is represented in memory and the word is instantly recognized—but that instant recognition was based on some prior phonological processing. So words that were originally decoded come to be recognized as wholes, and words originally taught as wholes must be studied letter by letter in order to be instantly recognized. The phonics versus sight-word debate should be laid to rest.

The division of words into onset and rime is a psychological reality (Trieman, 1985). In the 1934 edition of *Reading and Literature in the Elementary School*, Paul McKee discussed activities to help children decode words and indicated that there was mixed opinion as to whether it was best to start with the initial letters and then add the end (*sa-t*) or to keep the final letters together and add the beginning (*s-at*). Expressing some uncertainty, he did take a stand and recommend the latter. Teachers were encouraged to do word activities in which they took a known word and then changed the initial letters—*hand, sand, band, grand, stand*. Amazingly, McKee recommended that phonics instruction include "other tools such as analogy." For example, when confronted with the strange word "meat," he may derive its pronunciation by proper associations gathered from the known words "eat" and "met" (p. 189).

McKee's intuitive understanding of the reading process in 1934 led him to recommend what researchers confirmed 50 years later. Syllables are the most distinct sound units in English, and children and adults find it much easier to divide syllables into their onsets (all letters before vowel) and rimes (vowel and what follows) than into any other units. Thus *Sam* is more easily divided into *S-am* than into *Sa-m* or *S-a-m*. It is easier and quicker for people to change *Sam* to *ham* and *jam* than it is to change *Sam* to *sat* and *sad*. The psychological reality of onset and rime confirms the age-old practice of teaching word families and spelling patterns.

Lots of successful reading is essential for readers to develop automaticity and rapid decoding (Samuels, 1988; Stanovich & West, 1989; Juel, 1990). The major observable variable that separates good readers from poor readers is that good readers read a lot more, and when they are reading, they recognize most of the words instantly and automatically. If you recognize almost all the words, an unfamiliar word gets your immediate attention and you will stop and figure it out. Lots of easy reading in which most words are immediately recognized is essential for both the development of instantly recognized words and the ability and willingness to decode the occasional unfamiliar word. Many factors—including topic familiarity, text and picture support, number of unfamiliar words, and teacher support—interact to determine how easy or difficult a particular book is for a particular child.

Children become better decoders when encouraged to invent-spell as they write   Children have been inventing spellings for years, but until recently, those inventions have not been valued in most classrooms. There is still controversy about how long to allow children to continue to invent-spell and whether or not children will move through the stages of invented spelling if they are not given any spelling instruction. Encouraging invented spelling, however, does seem to help children develop decoding skills. Clarke (1988) compared the effectiveness of invented spelling versus an emphasis on correct spelling in first-grade classrooms. The children who had invented spellings were superior to the others on measures of word decoding at the end of the year. Furthermore, this invented spelling and decoding connection was particularly striking for the children who had been designated as having low readiness at the beginning of the year.

There is no research base for the exclusive use of decodable text in beginning reading instruction   The first time you encounter an unfamiliar-in-print word, you don't recognize it immediately. You have to figure out what it is. You might decode it or you might hear someone pronounce it. The next time you see that word, you might remember having seen it, but you might not remember what it is. Again, you could figure it out or you could ask someone, "What's that word?" Depending on how many repetitions you need to learn words (and that varies greatly from child to child) and on how important and distinctive the word is (most children learn *pizza* and *dinosaur* with few repetitions), you will eventually get to the point where you "just know it." A sight word, like a good friend, is recognized instantly anywhere. Recognizing most of the word instantly—and only having to stop and figure out the occasional word—is what allows us to read quickly and fluently.

Children do need to learn to decode words, but there is a danger in having them figure out all—or almost all—the words as they are beginning to learn to read. The danger is that they will get in the habit of "sounding out" every word—and that is not how good readers read. During the last "Phonics Era," it was not uncommon to hear children who read like this:

I-t w-i-ll b-e a g—oo—d d—ay.

Many of these children had read these common words—*it, will, be, good,* and *day* many times and should have recognized them as sight words. But they had gotten into the habit of sounding out every word, and habits are hard to break.

Some phonics advocates want to restrict materials beginners read to include only words they can decode and the absolutely necessary sight words. They argue that this will give children lots of practice decoding and require them to use their decoding skills as they read. The call for decodable text is to a great extent a response to the irresponsible beginning reading texts of the last era, in which the demand for real literature and real authors resulted in reading books that even average readers couldn't read! Teachers and publishers are now realizing that beginning readers need meaningful text that they are able to read. There is research evidence to support providing children with lots of "readable text"—text they can read easily. But there are no studies that suggest children learn to read better when the text they are reading is restricted to only those words they have been taught to decode.

There Is No "Research Proven" Best Way to Teach Phonics

The question of how best to teach phonics is an important one, and quite difficult to answer. Historically, there are three kinds of approaches to phonics—synthetic, analytic, and analogic.

Synthetic phonics programs teach sounds first, and children read words that contain those sounds. When children have learned the short sound for *a* and the sound for *m, t,* and *b,* they read the words *am, at, mat, bat, tab, tam,* and *bam.* As more sounds are added, more "decodable" words are read. The first "stories" the children read contain only words with the sounds they have been taught and a few necessary high-frequency words such as *the, is,* and *on.* "Real" stories are read aloud to the children, but the stories they read are intended primarily to practice decoding. Children also write, but their writing is limited to the words that contain the sounds they have been taught. Decodable text generally plays a large role in synthetic phonics programs.

In 1997, Grossen summarized studies by the National Institute of Child Health and Development (NICHD) and claimed that these studies supported a synthetic phonics approach. In a review of these NICHD studies, Allington and Woodside-Jiron (1998) found, however, that their own data did not support the conclusion that synthetic phonics is best.

> Thus, the NICHD-supported researchers seem to acknowledge that an early emphasis on code-oriented activities enhances performance on both phonological awareness and pseudo-word pronunciations tasks but that such an emphasis did not produce reliable achievement gains on word reading or text comprehension. (p. 8)

Another review of one of these studies (Torgenson, Wagner, & Rashotte, 1997) also raises doubts about this conclusion:

> A second concern is that the gains in phonetic reading skill shown by these children in the group that received direct instruction in these skills did not translate into differential improvement in real-word reading ability. (p. 220)

The evidence for synthetic phonics suggests that the children given this type of phonics instruction become better at reading "nonsense words" but not at reading real words or at comprehension.

Analytic programs begin by teaching children some words and then helping children to "analyze" those words and learn phonics rules and generalizations based on those words. The phonics in most basal readers is analytic, and children read stories using sight words, context, and prediction as they are learning the phonics rules. Phonics is taught gradually over a longer period of time, and children are encouraged to read all kinds of text and write about all kinds of topics. Their reading and writing are not controlled by or limited to the sound they have been taught.

Analogic phonics is also based on words children have learned to read, but rather than being taught phonics rules, children are taught to notice patterns in words and to use the words they know to figure out other words. In an analogic approach to phonics, children would be taught that if you know how to read and spell *cat*, you can also read and spell *bat, rat, hat, sat*, and other rhyming words. Analogic phonics, like analytic phonics, is taught gradually, and children's reading and writing are not restricted just to the patterns that have been taught.

In addition to synthetic, analytic, and analogic approaches, Stahl, Duffy-Hester, and Stahl (1998) identify and review research on two "contemporary" approaches to phonics—spelling-based approaches and embedded phonics approaches. Spelling-based approaches included word sorting (Bear, Invernizzi, Templeton, & Johnston) and Making Words (Cunningham & Cunningham, 1992). They conclude that "both of these approaches seem to be effective as part of overall approaches to teaching reading (p. 347). Embedded phonics instruction occurs in the context of authentic reading and writing and is often associated with whole language instruction. There is currently not enough data to draw any conclusions about the overall effectiveness of embedded phonics instruction.

To explain their conclusion that there is no research-proven, most effective approach to phonics instruction, Stahl, Duffy-Hester, and Stahl theorized that:

> The notion that children construct knowledge about words may explain why the differences among programs are small. As long as one provides early and systematic information about the code, it may not matter very much how one does it. . . . If the information is similar, the learning should be as well. . . . If this information is made available to children, then it may not matter exactly how the instruction occurs. (p. 350–351)

Another possibility for the lack of a clearly superior approach to phonics instruction may lie in the individual differences among children. Some children are much quicker at becoming automatic at spelling and decoding words. Other children need much more work with letters, sound, and patterns and need to decode a larger portion of the words for a longer period of time. While context is used primarily for checking for most readers, children do rely more on context in the beginning stages, and some children's huge listening vocabularies allow them to make better use of context and whatever letter sounds they do know.

The activities described in *Phonics They Use* provide children multiple and varied opportunities to obtain the information they need to successfully decode and spell words. The activities have different focuses and proceed differently precisely because there is no best way to teach phonics. The activities are multilevel so that children at different points in their word knowledge and who need different amounts of information can all learn something about how words work from the same activity. The activities all stress transfer because the only phonics knowledge that matters is what children actually do with that knowledge when they are reading and writing. There is no research-proven, best way to teach phonics but research does indicate that children who engage in a variety of phonics activities and in lots of reading and writing become better readers and writers.

REFERENCES

Adams, M. J. (1990). *Beginning to read: Thinking and learning about print.* Cambridge, MA: MIT Press.

Allington, R. L., & Woodside-Jiron, H. (1998). Adequacy of a program of research and of a "research synthesis" in shaping educational policy. (No.1.15). National Research Center on English Learning and Achievement, University at Albany, Albany NY.

Bear, D. B., Invernizzi, M., Templeton, S., & Johnson, R. (1996). *Words their way: A developmental approach to phonics, spelling, and vocabulary, K–8*. New York: Macmillian/Merrill.

Bryant, P. E., Bradley, L., Maclean, M., & Crossland, I. (1989). Nursery rhymes, phonological skills and reading. *Journal of Child Language, 16*, 407–428.

Clarke, L. K. (1988). Invented versus traditional spelling in first graders' writings: Effects on learning to spell and read. *Research in the Teaching of English, 22*, 281–309.

Cunningham, P. M. (1975–76). Investigating a synthesized theory of mediated word identification. *Reading Research Quarterly, 11*, 127–143.

Cunningham, P. M. (1979). A compare/contrast theory of mediated word identification. *The Reading Teacher, 32*, April, 774–778.

Cunningham, P. M. (1980). Applying a compare/contrast process to identifying polysyllabic words. *Journal of Reading Behavior, 12*, 213–223.

Cunningham, P. M., & Cunningham, J. W. (1992). Making words: Enhancing the invented spelling-decoding connection. *The Reading Teacher, 46*, 106–107.

Cunningham, J. W., Cunningham, P. M, Hoffman, J., & Yopp, H. (1998). *Phonemic awareness and the teaching of reading*. Newark, DE: International Reading Association.

Cunningham, P. M., & Guthrie, F. M. (1982). Teaching decoding skills to educable mentally handicapped children. *The Reading Teacher, 35*, 554–559.

Daneman, M. (1991). Individual differences in reading skills. In R. Barr, M. L. Kamil, P. B. Mosenthal, & P. D. Pearson, *Handbook of reading research* (Vol. 2, pp. 512–538). White Plains, NY: Longman.

Ehri, L. C. (1991). Development of the ability to read words. In R. Barr, M. L. Kamil, P. B. Mosenthal, & P. D. Pearson, *Handbook of reading research* (Vol. 2, pp. 383–417). White Plains, NY: Longman.

Gaskins I. W., Downer, M. A., Anderson, R. C., Cunningham, P. M., Gaskins, R. W., Schommer, M., & the Teachers of the Benchmark School. (1988). A metacognitive approach to phonics: Using what you know to decode what you don't know. *Remedial and Special Education, 9*, 36–41.

Goswami, U., & Bryant, P. (1990). *Phonological skills and learning to read*. East Sussex, UK: Erlbaum.

Grossen, B. (1997). Thirty years of research: What we now know about how children learn to read: A synthesis of research on reading from the National Institute of Child Health and Development. Santa Cruz, CA: Center for the Future of Teaching and Learning. (www.cftl.org)

Hogaboam, T., & Perfetti, C. A. (1978). Reading skill and the role of verbal experience in decoding. *Journal of Verbal Learning and Verbal Behavior, 70*, 717–729.

Jorm, A. F., & Share, D. L. (1983). phonological recoding and reading acquisition. *Applied Psycholinguistics, 4*, 103–147.

Juel, C. (1990). Effects of reading group assignment on reading development in first and second grade. *Journal of Reading Behavior, 22*, 233–254.

LaBerge, D., & Samuels, S. J. (1974). Toward a theory of automatic information processing in reading. *Cognitive Psychology, 6*, 293–323.

McKee, P. (1934). *Reading and literature in the elementary school*. Boston: Houghton Mifflin.

McClelland, J. L., & Rumelhart, D. E. (Eds.). (1986). *Parallel distributed processing, Vol. 2: Psychological and biological models*. Cambridge, MA: MIT Press.

McConkie, G. W., Kerr, P. W., Reddix, M. D., & Zola, D. (1987). *Eye movement control during reading: The location of initial eye fixations on words*. Technical Report No. 406. Champaign, IL: Center for the Study of Reading, University of Illinois.

McCutchen, D., Bell, L. C., France, I. M., & Perfetti, C. A. (1991). Phoneme-specific interference in reading: the tongue-twister effect revisited. *Reading Research Quarterly, 26*, 87–103.

Mewhort, D. J. K., & Campbell, A. J. (1981). Toward a model of skilled reading: An analysis of performance in tachistoscoptic tasks. In G. E. MacKinnon & T. G. Walker (Eds.), *Reading research: Advances in theory and practice* (Vol. 3, pp. 39–118). New York: Academic Press.

Moustafa, M. (1997). *Beyond traditional phonics*. Portsmouth, NH: Heinemann.

Nicholson, T. (1991). Do children read words better in context or in lists? A classic study revisited. *Journal of Educational Psychology, 83*, 444–450.

Rayner, K., & Pollatsek, A. (1989). *The psychology of reading*. Englewood Cliffs, NJ: Prentice Hall.

Rumelhart, D. E., & McClelland, J. L. (Eds.). (1986). *Parallel distributed processing, Vol. 1: Psychological and biological models*. Cambridge, MA: MIT Press.

Samuels, S. J. (1988). Decoding and automaticity: Helping poor readers become automatic at word recognition. *The Reading Teacher, 41*, 756–760.

Seidenberg, M. S. (1987). Sublexical structures in visual word recognition: Access units or orthographic redundancy. In M. Coltheart (Ed.), *Attention and Performance XII: The Psychology of Reading*, 245–263, Hillsdale, NJ: Erlbaum.

Seidenberg, M. S., & McClelland, J. L. (1989). A distributed, developmental model of word recognition and naming. *Psychological Review, 96*, 523–568.

Stahl, S. A., Duffy-Hester, A. M. & Stahl, K. A. (1998). Everything you wanted to know about Phonics (but were afraid to ask). *Reading Research Quarterly, 33*, 338–355.

Stanovich, K. E. (1991). Word recognition: Changing perspectives. In R. Barr, M. L. Kamil, P. B. Mosenthal, & P. D. Pearson, *Handbook of reading research* (Vol. 2, pp. 418–452). White Plains, NY: Longman.

Stanovich, K. E., & West, R. F. (1989). Exposure to print and orthographic processing. *Reading Research Quarterly, 24*, 402–433.

Tannenhaus, M. K., Flanigan, H., & Seidenberg, M. S. (1980). Orthographic and phonological code activation in auditory and visual word recognition. *Memory and Cognition, 8*, 513–520.

Torgenson, J. K., Wagner, R. K., & Rashotte, C. A. (1997). Prevention and remediation of severe reading disabilities: Keeping the ear in mind. *Scientific Studies of Reading, 1*, 217–234.

Trieman, R. (1985). Onsets and rimes as units of spoken syllables: Evidence from children. *Journal of Experimental Child Psychology, 39*, 161–181.

Phonics No One Can Use

(Getting Ready for the Teacher's Phonics Test)

In the midst of the current phonics frenzy, various groups have decided it would be useful to test teachers' phonics knowledge. Unfortunately, the items on these phonics knowledge tests have absolutely nothing to do with how readers actually use phonics. The test items test knowledge of jargon and rules, and you could know all of this and be a lousy phonics teacher or know little of it and be a very effective phonics teacher. So if you or someone you know is about to be rounded up and taken down for the "phonics test," study this and you will do better (on the test).

- You may be asked to recognize words with things like inflected endings, derivational suffixes, bound and free roots, and compound words. This is not hard if you know what all this jargon means.

  Inflected endings are added to words to change where in sentences they are used. The most common inflected endings are *s, ing, ed, ly,* and *er, est* (comparative). It may help you to remember that the phrase *inflected endings* has three of them: the *ed* in inflec*ted*, and the *ing* and *s* on end*ings*.
  Derivational suffixes change the word meaning. The new word has a separate dictionary entry. The most common of these derivational suffixes include *less, ful,* and *er* (person).
  Roots are bound if they are not words by themselves. They are free when they are words by themselves. The word *telegraph* has a bound root, *tele,* and a free root, *graph.*
  Compound words such as *homework* and *playground* are combinations of two words—both of which are free morphemes.

- You may be asked to count syllables and morphemes. Syllables are easy to count, but your answer might be wrong depending on your dialect. To count syllables, say the words and pretend you are Dan

Rather, Tom Brokaw, or Peter Jennings. Morphemes are a little harder, but focus on root words, prefixes, suffixes, and endings—remember there can be multiples of these. *Believe* has one morpheme (the *be* in believe is not a morpheme); believer = 2; believers = 3; unbelievers = 4.

- You may be asked to count speech sounds. Again, this is tricky because most of us speak a regional dialect. In my New England dialect, *park* has only three speech sounds (New Englanders don't do *r*'s), whereas Jim (husband) insists it has four. Use the "pretend you're a TV anchor" strategy and Jim is right. To determine speech sounds, ignore letters and talk anchorese and count (and pray!). Here are a few examples: ax = 3; coil = 3; sing = 3; think = 4; brought = 4; shine = 3; through = 3; spacious = 6.

- The schwa vowel in an unaccented syllable sounds kind of like "Uhh." The schwa sound is underlined in these words: a̲lone, har-m o̲ny, extra̲, cele̲brate, vacati̲on.

- Consonant blends are two or more consonants in which you can hear both sounds blended. The word *blend* begins and ends with a consonant blend. *Squall* and *scrub* begin with blends. *Burst* ends with one. *Bumpkin* has one in the middle. The words *comb* and *down* have two consonants at the end, but they are not blends because you only hear one of them.

- Consonant digraphs are two letters with a single sound—*ph* (as in digra*ph*), *sh, ch, th, wh*. The tricky part here is that silent letters don't count. *Write, knock,* and *gnu* do not begin with digraphs. *Ck* never begins a word but ends lots of short vowel words, such as *sick*.

- *C* and *g* are sometimes pronounced like *s* and *j* when followed by *e, i,* or *y,* as in *cent, city, cyclone, gentle, gist,* and *gym*.

- Long vowels (vowels that "say their names") can be spelled lots of ways. If you are asked to think of all the ways you could spell a vowel such as long *a*, think of words you know such as *rain, base, they, tray, eight, break,* and *vacation*. Remember that other vowels can spell the sound you are aiming for, as in *they* and *weigh,* and think of polysyllabic words, as in *vacation*.

- If you are asked to think of ways you can spell a consonant, again think of words you know with that sound—not that letter. The /K/ sound occurs in *cat, kids, rock, chaos, ax,* and *quiet*.

- There are six common syllable types in English:

    Open syllables end in a vowel and often have a long vowel sound—the *ti* in *tiger*.

Closed syllables end in a consonant and often have a short vowel sound—the *Tig* in *Tigger*.

R-controlled syllables end in an *r*, as in *carpet*.

Vowel-team syllables have two vowels together, as in *reason*.

Silent *e* syllables end in silent *e*, as in *decide*.

Consonant *le* syllables end in consonant *le*, as in *table*.

- You may be asked what you do with the *y* when adding endings. Just think of words like *try*. You change the *y* to *i*, as in *tried* and *tries*, except when adding *ing*—*trying*. If there is a vowel before the *y*—*play*, *destroy*—just add the ending.

- If you have to explain why there is a double *m* in *comma*, explain that the first *m* closes the syllable, thus assuring its short vowel sound. With only one *m*, it would have the long sound, as in *coma*.

- Words of Greek origin can be easily recognized by their *y*, as in *Olympics*; their *ch*, as in *choir*; their *ph*, as in *phonics*; and Greek roots such as *psyche* and *ology*.

Passing such phonics knowledge tests may be mandated, but that doesn't mean that knowing this stuff makes you a better teacher generally or even a better phonics teacher. While some studies have reported that many teachers fail such tests of phonics knowledge, no studies demonstrate that teachers who pass such tests actually can and do teach more effectively or even teach phonics more effectively. If these tests threaten in your area, ask for the "scientific" evidence that acquiring such knowledge improves teaching or learning.

INDEX